Kelvin

So good to make .
after all these years!
Enjoy the book. The front
cover pic was taken 31
years ago!
All best,

A Sporting Life

Chris Twort

A Sporting Life
by Chris Twort

First published 2016
by Chris Twort Books

Second Edition (3rd Printing) - December 2019

ISBN 978-1-5262-0499-8

A catalogue copy of this book is available from the British Library.

Printed and bound by St Andrews Press of Wells.

Whilst every effort has been made to trace the owners of the copyright material reproduced herein, the author would like to apologise for any omissions and will be pleased to incorporate any missing acknowledgements in future editions.

Dedicated to

My late parents, Kay and Nev –
always there for me.

My brother Richard –
for whom I have great admiration,
particularly as a successful businessman.

Clare and Phil –
for their great friendship and unfailing good advice.

George, Malcolm and John –
who all made highly significant decisions
to influence my professional and sporting life.

Foreword

This book is the fulfilment of a long-held ambition and I am so pleased it has now come to fruition.

Although I never hit the heights as a player (although I did manage one appearance behind the stumps for the Somerset 2nd XI), I like to believe and hope that I have an interesting story to tell.

You will read about coaching sport in both the state and private sectors, 27 overseas cricket tours, 14 years as an England U15 cricket selector – and even one or two scrapes I've got myself into, before (mostly) extricating myself.

Very grateful thanks to Tim Wood and Iain MacLeod-Jones at St. Andrews Press for all their help and advice.

Enjoy!

Addendum: After several requests for a copy of my out-of-print book, I decided to do not just a re-print but to add three chapters.

I hope you enjoy this Second Edition.

Photography credits
Debbi at Eric Purchase Photography
The Weston Mercury
Janette Tuckwell
Sarah Champion
Keith Curtis
Julie at Photos Unlimited
Malcolm Broad, MBE
Mike Fear
Mike Turner-Welch
William Sykes
Harold Skane
Paul Wickham
Olan Mills Photography UK
Marc Smeed
Belinda Wong
Chris Rew
Back cover photo by Georgina Hunter

Contents

CHAPTER 1
Where It All Began

I suppose my lifelong interest and indeed fascination in sport first surfaced when I was around four or five years old, living with my parents, Kay and Nev, and younger brother Richard in an area of Bath called Odd Down.

In the summer of 1951 I had 'gone missing' and a fairly frantic search was mounted. The reason for panic and foreboding was because a certain John Straffen was at large in the city. Straffen was under suspicion of having murdered two young local girls earlier that summer and was being sought by the police. After a couple of hours searching in the Odd Down area by family, friends and neighbours, I was eventually discovered sitting on the boundary edge at Hampset Cricket Club, a few hundred yards from my home in Bloomfield Rise, totally absorbed in the match taking place. John Straffen, incidentally, killed again in 1952 (his third murder) and was sentenced to death. Reprieved because of his mental state, he had his sentence commuted to life imprisonment and he remained in prison for more than 55 years until his death, aged 77, in 2007.

I recall little in the way of sporting activities at the two primary schools I attended in Bath – though I do recall a games competition in a field on Rush Hill when I was convinced I had won a prize, but was told I hadn't. There was also

Bedtime for brother Richard and I. Notice the early interest in cars (and identical pyjamas!)

a Bath & District Athletics event at the Recreation Ground (where Bath Rugby play), when it rained all day and was abandoned. It also rained for most of the day on 2nd June 1953 for the Queen's Coronation, when we crowded round a neighbour's television to watch those grainy, black and white pictures. Only a privileged few owned a TV set in those days.

The only other event of any significance I can recall occurred on a hot Friday afternoon in July when I was about seven or eight years old. We had just broken up from school for the six week summer holiday when I managed to pull an old railway truck on top of me while playing on my own in a quarry about half a mile from home. My father was working on his (very) second-hand car close by and, hearing my screams, ran down to see me trapped underneath the truck. He lifted it up and yelled at me to crawl out, which I did. My right arm, while not exactly hanging off, had 'burst open' with blood pouring out. My father gathered me up in his arms and ran to the crossroads adjacent to the quarry entrance. A bystander 'phoned for an ambulance from a handily placed kiosk but, before it arrived, a kindly gentleman said he would take me and my father to the nearby St. Martin's Hospital in his 'posh' car – very few around in those days of post-war austerity. My mother had come running down the road from home on hearing the news and, bless her, seemed more worried about my getting blood over the leather seats of the car than about my welfare or prospects of opening the England bowling at Lord's in years to come. I suppose I was lucky that my arm hadn't been severed, but the surgeon did a great job. I had to spend eight nights in hospital, had my arm encased in plaster until mid-September and still bear a distinctive scar to this day. My father went back to the quarry the day after the accident and couldn't lift the offending truck more than an inch or so off the ground; blind panic had given him the strength to raise it high enough to enable me to crawl out. And where was Health & Safety/Risk Assessment when you needed it?

CHAPTER 2
Sport at School

On the family moving to Weston-super-Mare in 1956, I attended Worle Junior School and 'enjoyed' my first real taste of competitive sport, playing in goal for the school football team. We were pretty awful and in the very first match lost 8-0 to Uphill Primary School, a certain Gordon Robert (currently Chairman of Weston Golf Club and who I met up with at a school re-union quite recently) scoring six of the goals. My brother, a scheming inside-left in the team, advised me at half-time to try doing something else – or words to that effect.

Aged 11 at Worle Junior School

I began eight years at Weston-super-Mare Grammar School for Boys in September 1957. The Girls' Grammar School was across the main driveway and this 'dividing line' was guarded by prefects. Anyone caught crossing the line was put in detention or worse . . . . It was around this time that a group of sixth formers put the school up for sale in the local paper - the Weston Mercury - describing it as a desirable residence, filled with a collection of old Victorian Masters!

Games at the school comprised mainly rugby in the Autumn and Spring Terms, followed by cricket (and some athletics) in the summer. There was also the annual cross-country run (House points on offer and a doctor's certificate required if you didn't fancy it), with the course set out through the sand dunes, along the beach (mud flats) and across some soggy fields. I had good stamina and usually finished in the first five, the aforementioned Gordon Robert the winner more often than not.

From the 2nd Form (Year 8) upwards, I was the regular full-back in the school rugby team in the days when that position merely demanded catching the high ball, kicking to touch and being the last line of defence. Two rugby injuries come to mind – a broken nose (blood everywhere) against the redoubtable St Brendan's College just before taking mock 'O' Levels (remember them?) and concussion (I think) about a year later when I was taken off and propped up against a tree in a match against Sidcot School. Very little gave me more pleasure when, in my

Receiving the Cricket Cup from Sir Ronald Gould, General Secretary of the NUT,
on Speech Day at Weston-super-Mare Grammar School, Nov. 1964

final year at school, I was awarded Rugby Colours after completing a full season in the 1st XV. This only came about because a certain Roger Webber transferred to Millfield School on a Sports Scholarship, leaving the full-back berth open for me. Roger, who I'm still in touch with, was, like Gordon Robert, a multi-talented sportsman who, after playing in one of the great Millfield teams (Gareth Edwards, JPR Williams, et al), went on to play almost 100 matches for Weston-super-Mare RFC 1st XV. He also played around 450 matches for Weston Cricket Club's 1st XI. By the way, that vintage Millfield team of 1964-65 not only won all 15 matches played but even won the Somerset Sevens MEN'S Tournament at the end of that season.

I was in the school Cricket 1st XI for four seasons (captain in the last two), as a wicketkeeper and lower order batsman. My final year, in 1965, saw the introduction of a certain Brian Rose, aged 14, into the team. Our unbroken 9th wicket partnership of around 40 runs (Brian got most of them) to defeat Millfield 2nd XI by 2 wickets stayed long in the memory – and still does! In those days, even at school, there was not a great deal of real coaching; though there was a regular Saturday afternoon fixture list for all the teams, something long gone in state schools. As a 'keeper I was reckoned to have good hand/eye co-ordination and didn't drop much. However, I used to take the ball crocodile jaw-like and only in later years did I turn the hands round to take the ball properly. You see, nobody ever coached me into taking the ball in the right way. As a young batsman, I used to play back to almost every ball until a teacher at the school, Graham Mitchell, taught me to play forward. Graham, who taught physics at the school, was an area selector for the County Schools' U15 team and in 1961 Roger Webber and I were chosen to play in the five matches against Cornwall, Devon, Gloucestershire, Hampshire and Bristol Schools. Two other boys from the school – Pete Kemp and Keith Tucker – were also selected, so the school was well represented that year. Also in that side was Alan Parsons, whose future sons, Keith and Kevin, were players in my Somerset U13 team in 1986, with Keith, of course, going on to have

Captain of Weston-super-Mare Grammar School 1st XI in 1965.
Front row, far left, is Brian Rose, later to become Somerset's most successful-ever captain
with five 1-Day trophies in as many years.

5

Somerset Schools' U15 Cricket Team, 1961.
I'm in the front row, 2nd left. Next to me in the centre is Alan Parsons, father of Keith and Kevin.
At each end of the back row are Graham Mitchell (left) and Bill Andrews (right).

an outstanding First Class career with the county. I'm not sure whether Gordon Robert even went for the trials (though possibly selected in 1962), as he was already making a real name for himself as an outstanding schoolboy golfer and hockey player. When I was 18 I played for the Somerset Youth (U19) team, under the irrepressible Bill Andrews. Bill had been a Somerset regular before and after World War 2, taking 750 wickets, but had the dubious distinction of having been sacked four times by Somerset as both player and coach. Bill always preferred the word 'encouragement' to the word 'coaching'. Certainly, nowadays, I know what he was trying to say.

CHAPTER 3
Fear of the Water

When I was about nine years old, still living in Bath, the family had a day trip to Weston-super-Mare (as one did in those days) and we ended up at 'The Pool' on the sea front. Some years later 'The Pool' became the 'Tropicana', but since about 2000 it has been a derelict, decaying shell, the local council forever dithering about what to do with it. However, in August and September of 2015, it gained world-wide publicity – and certainly put Weston on the map – when Banksy turned it into 'Dismaland'.

To return to that almost fateful day trip . . . . Although I could not yet swim, there was a rather inviting chute which I cheerfully slid down into about 12 feet of water. I somehow got to the surface and struggled out with the help, if I remember correctly, of an attendant with a long pole. I'm convinced that episode finished me forever where water is concerned.

Weston-super-Mare's lido pool in the 1960s

We had swimming lessons at the junior schools I attended and Weston Grammar School, but it was no good, the damage had been done as far as swimming was concerned. I used to dread the weekly trip to the local baths at Knightstone. They tried to convince me I could just lie back and float on top of the water, but I just knew that I would sink like a stone. My wise father asked a family friend, Bob Kent, to try and teach me to swim, reasoning that it might save my life, or someone else's, one day. Every Sunday morning Bob would arrive at our home and take my brother and I down to the local baths. As that weekly date got closer the feeling of dread just got worse, but on the odd occasion when Bob couldn't make it for some reason the relief was palpable – though I tried not to show it. I think we all knew it wasn't going to happen when I was about 14 and I even gave up the scouts because, to get through Stage 2, or whatever it was called, you needed to be able to swim a width of the baths.

In later years, when undertaking overseas Cricket Tours, I always listened pretty intently to the safety drill announcement, particularly the bit which begins, 'In the event of the aircraft having to alight on water . . . . . ' and had a 'sneaky' look to check that my life vest was indeed under my seat. This always seemed more pertinent on those 30/40 minute flights between the islands of the Caribbean. Unless it was essential, I always avoided boat trips of any sort and used to joke that the smallest vessel I would get on had to have at last three funnels. However, on Friday 1st April, 2005 (a date forever etched in my memory), we had to cross the Essequibo River in Guyana to play a cricket match on a Regional Tour. When we arrived to make the forty minute crossing in a boat, which would have struggled to meet Health & Safety standards almost anywhere on earth (not to mention a Risk Assessment), we were confronted by a floating jetty that appeared to be moving around the boat – I kid you not. Anyway, we made it to the match; perhaps unsurprisingly, it was our only defeat of the tour. The thought of the return journey across that brown coloured river at the end of the day might just have affected our performance. It certainly did mine and I was only the scorer.

So I never learned to swim and this has always been a matter of considerable regret and indeed sorrow.

CHAPTER 4

St Luke's

After eight years at the Grammar School, the next three were spent at St. Luke's College in Exeter, training to be a schoolteacher. The College had a sporting tradition/reputation, rather like Millfield, with my colleague, Angus Bentall, referring to it more as a P of E institution than a C of E one! For all three years, I lived in the same room in Baring Court, a Hall of Residence that had, apparently, been hastily erected pre-war as a temporary structure. It's no longer there now but was not demolished, so I hear, until long after I had departed. St. Luke's was an all-male institution, although 'mature' women students were about to be admitted. Rolle College in Exmouth, ten miles away, was our 'sister' college, but my thoughts and desires were more directed towards the nurses' quarters at the Royal Devon and Exeter Hospital and St Loyes College for Occupational Therapy.

I played rugby for various college teams over the three years and was even asked to captain the Freshmen's XV in my final year. I have great memories of frequently travelling with the 1st XV – a real force to be reckoned with in those days – to midweek matches in South Wales (by coach) and to Saturday fixtures (usually by train) for games in London. For the latter, it was a case of catching (hopefully) the last train back to Exeter, arriving in the (not so) early hours of Sunday morning. The highlight of the season was always the 'mini Varsity match'

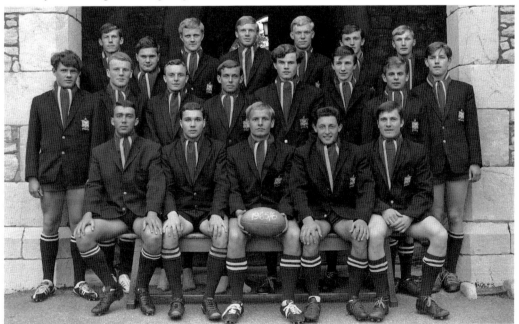

Freshmen's XV at St Luke's College, 1965-66.
I'm in the middle row, 4th right.

on a Wednesday in late February between St. Luke's and Loughborough Colleges. This took place at Old Deer Park, Richmond, on the outskirts of London, to where London Welsh have now returned after their brief stay in the Premiership. These matches were always fiercely contested and I'm delighted to recall that St. Luke's won all three encounters during my time there. A square-jawed Dan Baxter was a stalwart of the 1st XV – he always led the after-match singing, never in tune – and look how well his son Rob is now doing as Head Coach of Exeter Chiefs.

I played cricket at college mainly in my first and third years. In the middle year I used to travel back every Saturday in May and June to play for my then club, Uphill Castle. However, at the end of August that season I was incredibly upset when, over the Bank Holiday weekend, I was selected for just a 2nd XI match on the Saturday, while someone who had apparently just turned up and asked for a game was selected for the 1st XI on the Saturday, Sunday and Monday. I told them what I thought, left in a huff and joined the Weston-super-Mare club over the road. As in most things in life, time is a great healer and for many years now I have been a Vice-President at Uphill Castle (where my brother is an Honorary Life Member).

During my final term at St. Luke's we were playing a match at the 'Cat and Fiddle' ground in Exeter, had taken nine opposition wickets and were desperate to finish the game and go back to watch Manchester United v Benfica at Wembley in the European Cup Final. However, I don't think we ever got that final wicket – you could have drawn matches in those days – so we missed about the first twenty minutes of the final. Football wasn't at all tribal in the sixties, so everyone wanted United to become the first English team to win the European Cup. At almost the very end of 90 minutes, with the score at 1-1, Eusebio burst through, seemingly to score the winner, but shot straight into the tummy of the advancing Alex Stepney. George Best put United ahead in the first minute of extra time and they ran out 4-1 winners. This was 1968 and just ten years after the horrors of the Munich Air Disaster when eight United players lost their lives. On a cold, damp night in February 1958, thousands lined the streets of Manchester as the hearses brought them back from the airport.

George Best was undoubtedly the greatest footballer I ever saw live although, more recently, Thierry Henry has run him pretty close. Best could do the lot - pass and shoot with either foot, dribble, tackle, head the ball . . . and toy with the opposition. Also, in those days, pitches were mud heaps for most of the season when compared to the Emirates-like surfaces of today. And skilful players like Best didn't get the protection from referees that they do now. Players were more likely to get booked for dissent than for a reckless challenge. For six consecutive seasons, Best was United's top scorer, this despite being a winger. What a tragedy it was that the only thing that eventually beat him was the demon drink.

CHAPTER 5
Early Teaching Posts

In the spring of 1968 I secured my first teaching post, at Uphill Secondary School, only about a mile or so from where I lived. It was mainly to teach English, but I knew they wanted someone to assist with boys' games so was delighted to arrive at the interview to find that the other five candidates were female. Head of Boys' Games was Gerry Williams, who was fantastic to work with and frequently let me have the 'A' group while he took the 'B' pupils or 'strappers' as he used to call them. Gerry was a superb rugby threequarter (mainly in the centre) for both Weston-super-Mare and Somerset, when county rugby was very strong. I would bracket Gerry with Robbie Hazzard as comfortably Weston's best players in the last sixty years. 1968-1971 were the three years when we had British Summer Time all the year round, as an experiment, so were able to play inter-school matches during the autumn and spring evenings, leaving the weekends free. To me, the experiment worked and I would never have gone back to changing the clocks twice a year. Apparently, they did so because hens in Scotland stopped laying eggs, or some such reason.

Milton Junior School - Weston-super-Mare & District 6-a-Side Football winners, 1977

In 1971, Weston-super-Mare went comprehensive, so Uphill Secondary and the Boys' and Girls' Grammar Schools became Broadoak School. Don Thomas had been an excellent Head at Uphill Secondary but the new Head at Broadoak struggled to cope. When I introduced myself to him as i/c Cricket and complained that females in high-heeled shoes were regularly seen walking across the cricket square (not roped off), his reply was, "Ah, cricket, good game I'm told." Somewhat discouraging.

I decided to go into primary education and spent five terms from September 1972 at St. Martin's Junior School in Worle on the outskirts of Weston-super-Mare. Leslie Bull was the Headteacher – he had been my first Head as a pupil when the family moved from Bath in 1956 – but we never really hit it off and I certainly wasn't a great fan of team teaching (in vogue at the time).

In April 1974 I secured what turned out to a great move when I went about a mile westwards to spend almost 17 years at Milton Junior School. Taking over from the legendary George Gillingham as i/c all the boys' games (football and cricket) in the school, I was soon arranging upwards of 50 football and cricket matches a year with local schools. Football matches took place at a playing field about a quarter of a mile away, which entailed crossing a very busy main road –

Milton Junior School Football Team - winners of the Area 6-a-Side Shield in 1990, my final year teaching at the school.

Milton Junior School Cricket Team - Cup Winners in 1989

and also which Health & Safety wouldn't allow nowadays. For cricket matches, I booked a pitch at a local recreation ground, which entailed shoe-horning eleven boys into two cars (which also wouldn't be allowed today). I also endeavoured, where possible, to have some 'B' fixtures for those of lesser ability, as well as some U10 fixtures. I also organised skills courses (in the school playground) in both football and cricket, which concluded with pupils taking basic tests and earning badges and certificates.

Milton Junior School were twice winners of the Weston-super-Mare & District 6-a-Side Football Shield, competed for by the 18 junior and primary schools in the area. On the first occasion, in 1977, we also won the South Avon U11 Schools' Cricket Cup to complete a notable 'double'. Apparently, we entered by mistake as we were not officially in the South Avon area; however, as we progressed in the competition, the organisers told me they didn't have the heart to throw us out. Good for them, though I have to say we weren't invited to defend our title the following year! This was the time when top sports coaches (of which I wasn't one) in the country were being lured to the Middle East with the promise of fat salaries. England Football Manager Don Revie was one of the most high profile examples. So, flushed with success, I put my head round the door of Headteacher Peter Townsend's office and said, "I've had this offer from the Arabs." Without looking up from his desk where he was writing, Peter's reply was swift and to the point – "Well, I should take it if I were you." I have to say, in fairness, that Peter was one of the better of the twelve Heads I served under in my teaching career. The competition hasn't been that great.

Father Christmas at Milton Junior School in the 1980s. A chat with me followed by a gift, all for 50p!

My first 'sporty' car - an MG Midget in British Racing Green

CHAPTER 6

Weston Juniors

When I started teaching at St. Martin's in September 1972, I was invited to take over as Team Manager of the Weston Juniors, a representative football team drawn from the junior and primary schools in Weston-super-Mare & District. I knew of the existence of this team, who had around eight fixtures on Saturday mornings from mid-January to April. Opponents were from similar towns in Somerset – Bath, Taunton, Bridgwater, Yeovil – and from the area around Bristol (the 'unwanted and unloved' Avon county did not come into being until 1st April – a singularly appropriate date – 1974).

The Hon. Secretary of Weston Juniors was a delightful, if mildly eccentric, schoolteacher by the name of Harold Skane – loyally supported by wife Margaret – who was on the staff at Banwell Primary School, a few miles from Weston, for many years. As Team Manager elect, I was replacing a fanatical and untidy looking Welshman, Idris Evans, who was moving on to pastures new. A superb classroom teacher, Idris was known to usually arrive late for the journey to an away match, gulping down a cup of coffee and eating a slice of toast and marmalade. The boys loved him as an inspirational motivator, so he was going to be a tough act to follow. Rather like anyone who had to follow Sir Alex Ferguson . . . . . . or Arsene Wenger.

Harold Skane arranged the fixtures and trials for the squad of around fifteen took place in October (after school and before the clocks went back). Home matches were played at Uphill Primary School, Bournville Junior School and Milton Junior School. None of these schools had nets on the goalposts, but this was rectified when I moved to Milton and we subsequently played all our home games at their Ewart Road ground. The team had long since played in West Ham United colours and I was very happy for this to continue. The Hammers had a reputation for playing good football 'in the right way' and it was only a few years since England's World Cup success and the hugely influential roles of Bobby Moore, Geoff Hurst and Martin Peters.

I managed Weston Juniors – who later became Weston Primary Schools - for nineteen seasons; for three of these campaigns we were outstanding, in another three we were weak and in the other thirteen about average. Our memorable years were 1979, 1982 and 1989 when we triumphed in the end of season 6-a-Side competition for teams we played during our regular programme of matches. Considering we selected from fewer than 20 schools – some very small – it was a great achievement to do well against the likes of Bath (40 schools) and Bristol (80 schools). I returned home from our 1989 success on Saturday 15th April and turned

Weston Juniors - Winners of the Regional 6-a-Side Cup in 1978-79.
A truly outstanding team who played some great football.

on the television, only to witness the tragic events unfolding at Hillsborough in the first few minutes of the Liverpool v Nottingham Forest FA Cup semi-final.

After Harold Skane's retirement in the early 1980s, I became Hon. Secretary as well as Team Manager. We started playing matches from mid-November as we had now begun entering the Southern Counties Cup, encountering some pretty stiff opposition. I had decided that the team needed more expert coaching than I could offer and the first to lend an experienced hand was former Weston-super-Mare midfielder Johnny Coles. I later arranged to have the sports hall at Worle School for an hour's training once a week, when Phil Taylor did a great job as

Tim Bass, Managing Director of John West Contractors, presenting sponsored shirts to the Weston Primary Schools' squad, 1989-90 season. Tim also gave much coaching input to the team.

coach. In later years, it was Tim Bass, whose son Jonathan was a star player in the team in the mid-eighties. Jonathan went on to play as an accomplished defender for Birmingham City, before plying his trade abroad and even finding time to be a male model with his heart-throb good looks. Well, if you've appeared on the centre double page of 'Cosmopolitan', you must have something about you – not that Jon (as he was now known) had very much about him in that particular shot!

We always had fully qualified referees appointed for our home games – the likes of Bob Keyes, Peter Hoddinott and Mike Winstone were unpaid regulars – while Angela Dando did a great job providing the after-match refreshments up at the school. In the last few years of my time at the helm, we always had a trip to Southampton on a Saturday in February or March, played Southampton Primary Schools in the morning, before going to watch a Division 1 (now Premier League) match at The Dell in the afternoon. All matches were reported (by me) in the local press and at the end of the season we had a Presentation Evening when players were awarded trophies and certificates in recognition of their season playing in the team.

Finally, one match will always stand out for me – and we lost it 8-1! It was in March 1984 and we entertained Bath Schools at Ewart Road. I had a pretty good side that year – or so I thought – until that day when we were totally outplayed by a superb Bath team. Their skipper was Paul Tisdale who ran the show from midfield, scoring a couple of goals and laying on others. I had an excellent goalkeeper that year in Mark Pettifer and, but for him, the final goals against column would have been well into double figures. Paul Tisdale went on to play a number of games for Southampton in the top flight, but for the past ten seasons has been a successful manager of League 2 side Exeter City, always having to work with a shoestring budget. Only Arsene Wenger, of the 92 league clubs, has been in charge longer. Paul was also – and still is – an accomplished cricketer who played for the West Region U15 team in 1988 and still turns out in local MCC fixtures. The Weston captain in that match was Gareth Taylor, who later had a decent career with a number of league clubs as a striker, notably Crystal Palace and Sheffield United.

Weston Primary Schools - Regional 6-a-Side Winners
1982 - Captain: Jason Lucas   *1989 - Captain: David Mitchell*

CHAPTER 7

Uphill Phantoms and Milton Nomads

When I started teaching in September 1968 I was approached by a certain Rosemary Evans (mother of Nick), who asked me if I would consider managing the local junior football team, Uphill Phantoms by name. A group of boys had founded the club themselves the year before, but now needed an adult to manage and coach the team. I was happy to do this and ended up doing so for the next ten years. The team played in the local 6-a-Side League on Saturday mornings between September and April. The problem was that matches were played on poorly drained grounds on the old Westland's site in Winterstoke Road where, incidentally, Weston-super-Mare FC now plays. So it was not unknown for the programme of matches to be called off for up to four or five weekends in a row, causing a real backlog of fixtures which had to be played on evenings in April.

A successful era managing Junior Football teams

In the autumn of 1969 the driving force behind the formation of an 11-a-Side league was a Mr. Ron Ellis, a local journalist and writer with a passion for football. Such a league for young players was previously unheard of in the Weston area (better known for its rugby) but the very first matches in the Weston-super-Mare & District Schoolboys' Sunday League took place on a Sunday afternoon in mid-November. Doug Atwell was the Chairman, Ron Ellis the General Secretary and I was the Treasurer (not a great appointment as I've never been much of an accountant). I entered Uphill Phantoms in the U14 Division and we won the first game fairly comfortably, away to Banwell Athletic. During the next year or so the league became established in just the two age-groups, U13 and U15. I only entered teams at U13 level, preparing them in a different U12 Saturday League – though the morning games did sometimes clash with my Weston Juniors commitments. My teams were generally successful, winning league titles and cup competitions, though we had great rivals in Westland (later to become Weston) Falcons, managed by David Perriman. We played home games on a narrow but flat pitch at Drove Road Recreation Ground, an excellent venue as it was very well drained. I reckon in a league of 14 teams, eleven were managed by the father of one of the players in that team. So it was in this aspect that Dave Perriman and I were at an advantage; neither of us had a son in our side so parents tended to trust us to be fair minded in our selection. We were also well organised, wanted the game to be played in the right way and so it was only natural that the best players around tended to be drawn to either the Phantoms or the Falcons. Some of the other managers didn't always see it that way.

Between 1971 and 1973 I had an outstanding goalkeeper in Ian Main. Ian had been adopted and his father Roy, a keen follower of Somerset cricket and rugby, was in great demand to be Chairman of the Benefit Committee of Somerset cricketers in the seventies and eighties. I took Ian to Bristol City and Bristol Rovers for trials but he eventually ended up at Exeter City, playing a number of first team games for them in the former Divisions 3 and 4. Ian then joined the Devon and Cornwall Constabulary, but tragically died – I believe it was a heart defect – when only in his late thirties. I only got to know about this very sad event when his funeral, held at a packed Exeter Cathedral, had already taken place.

We regularly had a Christmas Draw to increase League funds when member clubs were required to sell a minimum number of tickets. As Draw Promoter I received much help from a great chap in Mark Eastman, sadly no longer with us. At the end of the season we had a grand Presentation Event at the Winter Gardens Pavilion in Weston-super-Mare, when all teams were represented, even if they hadn't won anything. The 1972 and 1973 events were complete sell-outs of 800 players, parents and friends. We always had great difficulty in getting a well-known footballer to present the awards; Ron Ellis even travelled to Manchester in a vain attempt to get George Best, but only got as far as speaking to his agent, alas. Cup Finals at the end of the season were always preceded by a penalty shoot-out competition when each side in the division nominated one of their players to take part. Former West Bromwich Albion and Bristol Rovers goalkeeper Dick Sheppard regularly came down from Bristol to take part; and he always stayed on to watch the final. Dick was a top bloke and how sad I was when I heard of his death from a heart attack when only in his early fifties.

Meanwhile, the Woodspring Junior League was formed, covering a fairly wide area between Weston-super-Mare and Bristol. They went straight in with divisions in five age-groups between U11 and U15, playing matches throughout the weekend, except on Saturday afternoons. This was really the beginning of the end for the Schoolboys' Sunday League, as large clubs who ran teams in all the age-groups, quite naturally, wanted to compete in just one league. The Woodspring

League was well run by Les Ferris, the Chairman, and Chris Nelms, the General Secretary, while results were taken over the phone on a Sunday evening by Ron Moore. Rules (and fines) were strict and woe betide you if a player registration form or result card arrived late – or didn't arrive at all. However, one of the biggest bones of contention was where a player lived in relation to the club he wished to play for.

After Uphill Phantoms had been sadly, if inevitably, wound up, I was invited by Milton Nomads (founded by Ron Ellis) to manage their U13 team in the Woodspring League for the 1979-80 season. This was very handy as I was now living in Milton, a few hundred yards from their home ground at Baytree Rec. We had a decent season and I carried on in similar vein for the next couple of years. In 1982-83 I was lucky enough to have an excellent U12 team at Nomads and went on to take the same group of players through to U13, U14 and U15. We were very successful, winning league titles and cup finals, playing good football in all winds and weathers. Jason Lucas was an excellent captain in the back four all through these years, while I was lucky to have skilful and hard-working midfield players in Dean Cope, Danny Richards and Oliver Latchford (nephew of Everton striker, Bob Latchford).

For the 1986-87 season, I managed Nomads' U13 side, a pretty average outfit to be honest, but with a star player in Neil Ramsey, who was very quick, extremely skilful and who scored goals with either foot. He was a Derby thoroughbred in a field of selling platers. Unfortunately, Neil lived a few miles south of Weston in Burnham-on-Sea and the Woodspring League decreed, in their infinite wisdom, that Neil couldn't play for Milton Nomads because he lived 'out of the area'. I was furious with this ruling and, at the next league meeting, marched to the front with the trophies won by the club the previous season and plonked them down on the officials' table as a form of protest. I know I shouldn't have done it; the Woodspring League officials were equally furious at my action and called an Extraordinary General Meeting in an effort to have all Nomads' teams removed from the league. What had I done! This EGM was held at the Lord Nelson pub at Cleeve in early December 1986 when I had to stand up and make an impassioned plea for mercy. We survived, just, by the slenderest of margins, but if Les Ferris had had his way, we would have gone, rather like a certain Headmistress if she'd had her way nearly thirty years later.

The Woodspring League did ban me from any involvement in running teams in their league (still not sure if they could do that), but I'd learnt my lesson . . . . I think. I lost touch with Neil Ramsey after this sorry episode, though I did hear some years later that he'd become a highly talented and successful golfer.

After I had nearly caused the club to go out of business, I was delighted to have two successful years with Nomads' U11 team in the Bristol based Hanham Minor

League. In 1987-88 we finished third in the league and lost in the cup final 1-0 – to a hotly disputed goal – in a match played at Twerton Park in Bath. However, the following season, we won the league in style, being unbeaten, winning 28 and drawing two of the 30 matches. This was undoubtedly my greatest achievement as a junior football manager since, although we had an outstanding set of 10 and 11 year-old players, the other 15 sides in the league were all from the Bristol area and were nearly all decent, well-coached teams. I was fortunate to have a star striker in Brett Gready (92 goals) and a diminutive, highly skilled midfielder in Jamie Shore. Jamie later signed for Bristol Rovers and was looking likely to make the grade until a chronic knee injury forced a very premature retirement. He then took his coaching badges, worked with various clubs and is someone I'd like to meet up with to see how he's now doing. I was also fortunate in having a loyal and very reliable linesman in Glyn Dando.

In the penultimate game of that season we played our biggest rivals in a midweek home game. We edged it 2-1, the match being refereed by Ron Groves who, on the previous Saturday, had officiated at the Arsenal v Everton match at Highbury. Ron told me afterwards that he couldn't believe how high a standard the football had been; I reckon he thought it was going to be 20 little boys just chasing after the ball. After the final game of the season, on May Day in Bristol, we returned to the Weston-super-Mare ground, entered the clubhouse and were greeted by everyone standing up and applauding. You just live for moments like that . . . . makes it all worthwhile.

*Not looking at the camera after receiving a sports award from the
Mayor of Weston-super-Mare in 1990*

CHAPTER 8
The Move to Millfield

My professional career – indeed my entire life – began to change dramatically on Tuesday 24th July 1990. I was present at the Somerset Schools' U13 v London Schools cricket match at Edgarley Hall, as it was then known, when I was approached by the Edgarley Headmaster, George Marsh. He knew that I was keen to move into the independent sector and mentioned that a Year 5 class teacher (Bob Yetzes by name) was leaving that Christmas to take up a deputy headship. Bob's main sport was hockey, but George seemed pretty certain that he could fit me in. I was also aware that Edgarley's Head of Cricket, the legendary Bryan Lobb, was due to retire the following year, so . . . . .

On Saturday morning, 15th September, I drove to Edgarley for a 'job interview'. On arrival, George said I wouldn't be interviewed as such (wouldn't happen nowadays), but would just be shown around the school and introduced to senior staff. On the Monday morning he would ask them what they thought of me and their replies would determine whether I'd be offered the job. Anyway, I WAS offered the job and was due to start on Monday 7th January 1991. However I wasn't due back from my first West Indies Cricket Tour until Saturday the 12th. All was well, however, as George very kindly agreed that I could start a week late and so undertake the tour. So, in a very short time, George had given me a dream appointment and saved my tour. I have to say, however, I did suffer some gentle chiding from some staff when I turned up a week late with a nice tan.

During my first cricket season at the school I either looked after the U10s or accompanied Bryan Lobb with the 1st XI. The first time I ever took charge of an Edgarley team was with the U10s in an away match at Wells Cathedral Junior School on the first Saturday in May. We batted first and a disastrous first over ended with us 1 run for 2 wickets and the two star players (Wes Durston and Paul Heywood) both out. However two of the 'lesser lights' – Matthew Gower and Oliver Downes – came to the rescue and we eventually reached 147. By the time Wells batted, Wes and Paul were thirsting to get into the action. They tore in from their somewhat over-long run-ups and demolished the home side for just 29. Wes Durston was an obvious star in the making and later in the season took 7 wickets in a low scoring win against Hazlegrove.

The U10 wicketkeeper was Richard Williams, son of Vaughan, a highly talented rugby scrum-half. Vaughan, who had been in the year below me at St Luke's, was an outstanding schoolboy fly-half and played in that great Millfield side of 1964-65. Vaughan joined Bath, was selected for Wales 'B' and looked set for a good few years in the game – pre-professional, of course. However, he was kicked in the head when playing for Bath against Weston-super-Mare, with the result that Bath immediately cancelled all future fixtures with Weston. It wasn't the first time that Vaughan had suffered such an injury and he was advised to retire, when only in his mid-twenties. He remained somewhat bitter about events for many years, no doubt thinking of what might have been. As his House Assistant between 1993 and 1996, we had a major fall-out over 'policy', but I was pleased to 'kiss and make-up' in 2000 (the year he left the school) when I drove him to the Millenium Stadium for the Wales v Scotland Six Nations match. We had great seats (plus hospitality) and Vaughan even paid my parking fine.

Bryan Lobb's 1st XI in his final season was very strong, as was usually the case. He had a formidable, four pronged pace attack, comprising the skipper Dominic Brogan, Chris Kindon, Ben Morton and Ben Hollioake. They simply terrified most opposing teams into submission. Ben Hollioake was adored by the girls in the school with his film star looks (rather like Andy Tait nineteen years later), but it caught him out when we played at Monkton Combe in mid-May. Ben was apparently chatting up a girl (or girls) and missed the coach. Bryan Lobb was not amused and even though Ben persuaded the chaplain to drive him to the match

Edgarley Hall 1st XI 1988
Far right at the back is my predecessor Bryan Lobb. Far left is his faithful No.2 Mike Rutter

(arriving just in time), Bryan refused to let him play (having already recruited his replacement from the adjacent 3rd XI match) and made Ben watch the entire match from the boundary edge. A harsh lesson.

Six years later Ben (right) was playing for England at Lord's in an ODI against Australia – and scoring a brilliant 64 on his debut. England, by the way, won that mini-series 3-0. Happy days. Ben's death at the age of just 24 as a result of a road accident in Australia remains one of cricket's – and indeed sport's – greatest tragedies. Accompanied by Millfield Prep colleague Janette Tuckwell, I was privileged to attend Ben's Memorial Service at Southwark Cathedral in July 2002, when the tears still flowed, four months after the accident. A terrible loss.

When George Marsh gave me a teaching post at Edgarley Hall in the Autumn of 1990, it turned out that I was his final appointment, as soon after he announced that he was to be the new Head of Dulwich College Prep in south-east London as from September 1991. Just before the end of the Summer Term, George called me into his office to inform me that I would be Bryan Lobb's successor as Head of Cricket, as from 1st September. It was a dream come true. What made it even better was that I was Bryan's choice as well. George's successor as Head was to be Richard Smyth; he had a genuinely tough act to follow.

In June 1991, at the age of just 59, Colin Atkinson died after a lengthy battle with brain cancer. Colin first came to Somerset County Cricket Club from the north-east in 1960 and played as a leg-spinner and middle-order batsman. 'Boss' Meyer gave him a teaching job at Millfield, 'excusing' him during the Summer Term to play cricket. Colin captained Somerset between 1965 and 1967 before announcing his retirement from all cricket. Arthritic fingers had forced him to change from leg-spin to effective medium-pace, but he will always be remembered as an outstanding captain, able to get the best out of his players. In 1966 he led Somerset to third place in the County Championship while, in his final year, to the Gillette Cup Final at Lord's – where they narrowly lost to Kent. Colin was Headmaster of Millfield School from 1970, before being appointed Principal of Millfield Schools. I met Colin at a function at the County Ground in November 1990 and he kindly told me how delighted he was to hear of my appointment to teach at Edgarley. I remember thinking that his health seemed to have improved, but sadly it deteriorated rapidly in the New Year. Colin was an immense visionary where education was concerned and was the perfect successor to 'Boss' Meyer.

He was always willing to allow (free of charge) both Somerset Schools and West Region teams to use the 1st XI ground for matches and trials, instructing his Master i/c Cricket to ensure that we were 'fed and watered' (at no cost) and generally looked after. Colin was so highly thought of in top cricket circles that he was destined to become Chairman of the Test & County Cricket Board, now the England & Wales Cricket Board.

Between 1983 and 1985 I served under Colin's chairmanship on Somerset's prestigious Cricket Committee. Chairmen before and since only wanted former First Class players on this committee, but Colin told me he would value my expertise and knowledge of youth and schools' cricket. I was delighted to serve and it proved to be a fascinating three years.

No greater tribute to Colin Atkinson, CBE, could have been given than that by Dennis Silk in his superb address at Colin's Memorial Service in a packed Wells Cathedral on 4th October 1991. This address is re-produced in full on Pages 10-13 of the 1992 Somerset CCC Year Book. I've just re-read it and it brought tears to my eyes.

I suspect my appointment as Edgarley's new Head of Cricket didn't go down too well with some of the Games and Cricket staff. After all, I'd got the job after just two terms at the school. However, I was determined to get on with making my own mark and being successful. I started a Friday after-school cricket activity in the off-season for the juniors in the sports hall and it proved to be very popular. In fact, Rob Link remarked that it was just about the most popular of all the extra-curricular activities on offer. Rob did a great job for many years, organising and setting up these activities and since his retirement a few years ago has been sadly missed. He also carried out numerous 'unseen' jobs in the school and was a real pillar of the community. My cricket activity usually followed the lines of batting, bowling and fielding skills and always finishing off with a game of continuous/non-stop cricket.

The sports hall at the time was used for absolutely everything and, being the only large building in the school, sporting activities frequently had to take second place to examinations, meetings, plays, play rehearsals, musical events, concerts, theme days and so on. I remember Caroline Park, Head of Girls' Games, training her squad for the Nationals in the 'covered way' because the sports hall was in non-sporting use. Not what you would really expect in a top sporting school. The sports hall had a perfect 'carpet' floor and it was not until fourteen years after my arrival that it was replaced with a modern version with its very imperfect and far too slippery floor – not to mention numerous other imperfections. So the old sports hall became the assembly hall. Incredibly, I always thought, that too was given a slippery (expensive) wooden floor.

In the early nineties, Millfield employed Tony Corner (Old Millfieldian), Chairman of the Somerset Cricket Association, to assist me in coaching the first team. Tony was a fine coach and it was such a shock when he passed away in 1995 when only in his fifties. He has been greatly missed these past twenty years. When District cricket started for the Somerset age-group teams in the late nineties, they were known as 'Corners', in memory of Tony who had done so much on behalf of youth cricket.

The summer of 1992 (my first in charge) saw the 1st XI play a record number of 28 matches – "Who is this bloke?" I heard the Head of English mutter – losing only two, to the Cornwall County U13 side and to Wellesley House in the J.E.T. (Joint

Edgarley Hall Cricket team, winners of the Prior Park 6-a-Side Tournament in 1994.
At the foot is the head of skipper Wes Durston, now Derbyshire's 1-Day captain.
Notice the old Edgarley caps, with windmill, worn by two of the players.

Educational Trust) Final at Oxford. 11 year-old Alex Loudon took five wickets against us in that final; he went on to play for Warwickshire and even in a 1-Day International for England. After retiring early from professional cricket, Alex went into the City to earn far more money and was also romantically linked with Pippa Middleton, the Duchess of Cambridge's younger sister. Ah, the benefits of wealth, good looks and an Eton education.

Captain of the 1st XI in 1992 was Joey Barrington, son of six times World Squash champion, Jonah. Jonah, now in his seventies, still coaches the game at Millfield and remains, quite rightly, a revered figure there. Daniel Durston (Wesley's older brother) took 55 wickets in the season with his accurate away-swingers; this figure remained a record until 2015 when left-arm spinner Max Hancock took 56.

In 1993, Danny White captained the team. He had opened the batting the year before as a Year 7 ('B' Blocker) and scored exactly 1,100 runs in his two seasons in the 1st XI. He was a neat, uncomplicated opening bat who looked a near certainty for the England U15 team in 1995, but had a disappointing and somewhat unlucky Bunbury Festival and wasn't selected. Danny was also an excellent footballer but, like his older brother, John-Simon, suffered various knee injuries to impede his progress. Danny's father, John, founded 'Premier Trophies' about this time and has supplied all Millfield Prep's cups, shields and medals - which are numerous - ever since.

We lost, controversially, to Cumnor House in the J.E.T. semi-final by just one run, mainly due to a highly debatable umpiring decision off the penultimate ball of the match. It was one of the very, very few occasions when I've confronted the umpires as they walked off the field; shouldn't have done it but we were all pretty incensed.

One memory of 1993 was the block fixture at Clifton College Prep in mid-June when the girls commandeered our booked coach to go to a rounders fixture, leaving three cricket teams – including my 1st XI – without transport. Fortunately, Risk Assessment hadn't been invented so we travelled to Clifton in various modes of transport, including my sporty Nissan RX7. Will Jones was one of my passengers, scoring a match winning 70 odd not out, so my driving hadn't unnerved him too much.

Wesley Durston was the 1994 captain and he led from the front with runs and wickets in abundance. He was also a great fielder, especially in the slips – a real asset at this age-group and certainly not very common. He also took 50 wickets with his pace bowling to add to the 41 he took in 1993; in those days, not that far-off, bowling restrictions for young players hadn't yet come into place but, if they had done so, I am sure Wes would simply have turned to off breaks which he now bowls for Derbyshire as their 1-Day skipper (and hard hitting batsman). Later captains of the 1st XI – like Joe Becher, Max Waller and Nick Pang – followed the same route.

We didn't make the JET Finals that year but did win the last ever Prior Park Six-a-Side Tournament. We had 'A' and 'B' sides competing and the Bs came very close to beating their seniors, before Paul Heywood hit the penultimate ball of the match back over the bowler's head for four. Prior Park were desperate to win for their retiring Head, John Bogie, but we edged them out in a tense final.

The 1995 skipper was Liam Casey, a nice lad from the London area and one of the few who opted to play for my Somerset Schools' U13 team rather than for the county where he lived. Liam was an excellent opening batsman and good enough to tour the West Indies with the Regional U15 side in 1997, scoring a couple of half centuries into the bargain. For the first time this year I had help with running the team. 19 year-old Charlie Little, having just completed sixteen years in the Millfield system, rendered huge assistance in coaching the side. Charlie was a good cricketer himself and scored a century for my County U13 side in 1989. We were still trying to win the JET Shield again, having been the very first winners in 1986 (before my time), but we lost in the semi-final at Oxford. However, this year saw the start of a play-off match for 3rd/4th place and it was pleasing, at least, to conclude the season with a 9 wicket victory.

We were hot favourites to win the 1996 JET final but completely blew it, being bowled out for the first and only time that season. We needed to score only 110 to defeat Dulwich Prep but subsided to a miserable total of just 76. Mark Easter (Sale Sharks rugby player), brother of England Rugby international Nick, took 4-19 for Dulwich. We were captained by a hugely talented sporting all-rounder in Neil Goodman. Neil's primary school Headteacher in Wellington, David Martin – whose wife Christine was an excellent Head of Year at Millfield Prep – and myself pulled out all the stops to get Neil into the school in Year 7. Apparently, he'd been offered a free day place at Taunton Prep, but still came to us as a boarder at 50% off full fees. Neil was the first, but certainly not the last, top cricketer I 'persuaded' to come to Millfield Prep. His mum was set against Neil boarding, but I'm sure she came round when she saw what he was achieving. In fact, two years later he was playing with success for England U15s against India, along with his great pal Arul Suppiah. Another bonus for me was that Neil's father, Paul, was an excellent scorer for the 1st XI for two seasons.

I was involved in an unsavoury incident in the '96 season for which I could only admit, 'Guilty as charged'. Our regular wicketkeeper, Rob Hawkins, was supposed to be swimming for the school in a Prep Schools' competition in Bromsgrove, despite the fact that he'd left the swimming squad at Easter. However, I, Rob and his mum were all rather keen for him to play in a JET quarter-final match at St.

Bede's in Eastbourne. So a devious plan was hatched in that Rob cried off sick that day and we picked him up at a Little Chef on the A303. We won the match fairly easily on a playing area about the size of the centre court at Wimbledon, but next day there was hell to pay for yours truly. I had a very sticky twenty minutes with Sarah Champion (Acting Head, who had taken over from Richard Smyth – unable to cope with the pressure – the previous September). I received a 'Written Warning', stating that this whole sorry episode brought into question my suitability to be in charge of a major sports department in the school. Strong stuff. I also had to write a letter of apology to Head Swimming Coach, Helen Gouldby.

Helen is still at the school and I am sure she has now forgiven my severe indiscretion twenty years on. I am pleased to confirm that she continues to do a fantastic job at Millfield Prep, one of her most recent successes having been World champion James Guy. She and husband Sam have two daughters – Alice and Charlotte – who are both, I gather, outstanding swimming prospects. Rob Hawkins, by the way, has gone on to have a successful rugby career with Bath, Leicester and now Newcastle; all this after having part of his ear bitten off while playing for Bath Youth against Cardiff Youth. Enough said!

CHAPTER 9
The Simon Cummins Years

Simon Cummins, aged just 36, was the school's new Headmaster in September 1996. He made it clear to Heads of Sport that he expected/demanded national titles should be won, with no excuses! He would bring in top performers from other schools to achieve this, offering huge monetary awards to persuade parents to send their offspring (usually boys in those days) to Millfield Prep, which the Marketing Department recommended that the school should now be called. I'm sure that this contributed to Simon's eventual downfall four years later. He once told me that no Millfield team in whatever sport should ever lose to a state school team. When I put it to him that my U11 football team often struggled to compete against a primary or middle school side – who usually played football and little else all the year round and whose players were often members of a local club side where they would get decent coaching – he was still having none of it. Simon used to revel in the Monday morning assemblies, giving out trophies and medals to successful sports teams at inter-school, county, regional and national levels. It was like an Annual Prizegiving taking place once – and sometimes twice – a week.

In 1997, for the first time, there was to be a National cricket competition (the Calypso Cup) for school U13 teams (the 40 county U12 winners from the previous year). A chirpy young man called Joe Becher – who, ironically, later worked under Simon Cummins at Odgers in London – was 1st XI captain and we also had a young James Hildreth in the team.

We set out on the road to Headingley, where the Calypso Final was to be played, on Thursday 1st May with a visit to QEH, Bristol. The temperature that day at Failand reached 25°C and was also the very day that Tony Blair achieved a landslide General Election victory. We won the match by 7 wickets and celebrated – not for the first time and it wouldn't be the last – at McDonald's. For the next couple of weeks we had almost non-stop rain and had to play the second round of the Calypso Cup over the road at Edgarley Manor on the artificial pitch.

In the quarter-final we played Cape Cornwall School at St. Just Cricket Club on a wet and windy Tuesday at the end of the annual Cricket Tour to Devon and Cornwall. They fancied their chances and were led by future West Regional captain, Jason Hall. However, a superb 70 odd from Joe Becher saw us to a comfortable success. Stuart Coates and I drove the minibuses back to school in pouring rain.

The next day, however, dawned fine and sunny and we set off to play a friendly match away at Cheltenham College Junior School. We batted first, I was umpiring and we were about 40 minutes into our innings when I was alerted to a drama which was unfolding on the adjacent pitch. The players had left the field and two paramedics were desperately trying to revive a 12 year-old Cheltenham player who had collapsed after a spell of bowling. The boy, Alexander Edwards, was taken to hospital and all matches taking place were, quite rightly, immediately abandoned. Alexander died a week later at the John Radcliffe Hospital in Oxford; the most terrible of tragedies. Simon Wynn, who had been in charge of our team in that match, represented the school at the funeral.

So we reached the last four of the Calypso Cup and on Monday morning, 23rd June, set out to play King's College Junior School, Wimbledon, in the semi-final. Stuart Coates was with me, kindly agreeing to drive the minibus, as I had been somewhat unfairly branded in the staffroom as someone who burned out minibus clutches. "You can't drive them in the same way as you drive your boy racers, Tworty."

It was the first day of Wimbledon tennis – just up the road – so, predictably, rain showers were never very far away. We agreed on 25 overs a side and on losing the toss were inevitably put into bat. After seven beautifully bowled overs from the King's opening attack we were 13-0 and I later congratulated our openers – Joe Becher and Mark Agutter – on not panicking over the lack of early runs. We got to 141-9 and then dismissed the home side for 77. We were through to Headingley on 10th July in the first-ever National U13 Final.

We stayed overnight at a Travelodge near Oxford, ready to try, once again, to win the JET Shield on the Tuesday at St. Edward's School. It was certainly our day as we comprehensively defeated hot favourites Wellesley House by 7 wickets with overs to spare, James Hildreth spanking the ball to the leg-side boundary for the winning runs. Ever since we had left school the previous morning, Stuart had never quite trusted the minibus and the engine duly gave out as we were going under a bridge leaving Oxford to get onto the A34. My immediate thought was not that we would be pretty late back, but rather how lucky it was that I wasn't the driver! Stuart took the players to the Little Chef over the road and told them to order what they liked – part necessity/part celebration – while I called Foundry Garage in Street. The food and drink bill came to around £130 (worth a lot more nowadays), but I was too happy to care after what we had achieved in the last two days. It was around midnight when we eventually did arrive home.

The following week, we again won the County Shield – which had to be replayed after we had Ansford School 50-8 at the County Ground and it rained – so a win at Headingley would give us a unique treble. As Thursday 10th July was in the first week of the holidays (nowadays it's in the second), we travelled up independently the day before to stay at the Post House Hotel in Brighouse (arranged by ESCA, paid for by Calypso). I brought up a couple of the players in my still sporty Nissan, but travelling up the M1 hit a thunderstorm of Biblical proportions in its intensity. It also landed at Headingley, which meant that the first Calypso Final had to be played on a hastily cut wicket just off the square.

Our opponents were the Royal Grammar School, Lancaster, an unknown quantity. They batted first and reached 47, using the short boundaries to good effect, before losing their first wicket. A remarkable spell of bowling from James Hildreth (7-6-1-1) pegged Lancaster back and they could only reach 122-8 off their 35 overs. We had done well. In our reply we lost both openers cheaply, but undefeated half-centuries from Luke Stokes and Matthew Young guided us to an 8 wicket victory and the treble. It was a poignant moment for Richard Stokes, Luke's father, terminally ill with Motor Neurone Disease. Richard had lost the power of speech, but could still smile with evident pleasure and satisfaction at seeing his son do so well on a Test match ground. Tim Harris always reckoned that Luke was technically the best young batsman he ever coached in his long career. In our cup winning team that day was Simon Mantell who, together with brother Richard, went on to have distinguished hockey careers with both England and Great Britain. In later years they occasionally returned to school to give talks and demonstrations. They have always been a huge credit to their parents, Chris and Ali, both former Millfield teachers.

Simon Cummins hadn't stayed in the hotel, but arrived just before the start, having caught the first train of the day from Temple Meads to Leeds. On arrival, he announced that he had spent his journey productively, signing off around 200 end-of-year school reports! As we were all about to depart at the end of a successful day I realised that I would be transporting Simon the 240 miles back to Somerset, as all the players would be travelling home with their parents. On the long journey south, I tried to tell him that it wouldn't always be as good as this (the unique treble), but he dismissed this pessimistic/glass half empty outlook, saying we could repeat our success in 1998, no problem.

It all began going downhill just two months later in mid-September when we lost the held-over County U12 final at the County Ground in Taunton to Chilton Trinity School from Bridgwater – a state school! – by 7 wickets. James Hildreth was out for a single, but the Chilton team did contain three future West Region players, including skipper Steve Davis who was named Man-of-the-Match. The 1998 school team, captained by James Hildreth, was weaker than usual. The skipper was way out the best player, scoring 821 runs – including three hundreds in four days in May – and taking most wickets with his pace bowling. Chilton Trinity defeated us, again, by 9 wickets in the County Shield Final. We did reach the JET Final, but Wellesley House gained revenge for a year earlier, winning by 25 runs. Josh Taplin was run out near the end to seal our fate and, on returning to the small pavilion, he threw his bat down and uttered an oath. An unhappy, glowering Simon Cummins heard it and told me to ban Josh from the next game . . . . . though not sure if there was one. Things were still going downhill.

On the morning of Saturday 8th May 1999, Simon called me into his office and told me we had 'come to the end of the line'. I could either leave now, pending an enquiry, or go quietly at the end of the term with a decent reference. Things had been building up against me, culminating in a pretty outrageous allegation made against me by a 'titled' pupil on behalf of his friend. Over aggressive physical punishment, apparently. What a joke.

I decided to see the term out, but news of my impending departure leaked out and was soon the talk of the school. We had a thoroughly decent side that year, which included four outstanding Year 7 pupils in Robin Lett, Sean Parry, James Barrowman and Harry Santa-Olalla. We had also qualified for the Calypso Cup. We were captained by the ultra-intelligent Richard Timms, the only skipper I have ever sacked (in August that year for Somerset U13s). Richard was a delightful opening bat with a superb technique and a more than useful leg-spinner, but he had great difficulty in taking and accepting advice/instructions from me or, indeed, anybody else. A few years later, Richard spent at least five years at Cambridge University, earning the reputation as a professional student.

On Wednesday 26th May we played Hazlegrove at home in the annual block fixture match. My mother was having a fairly major operation in Weston-super-Mare Hospital that day, so I was pleased when we put them in, bowled them out for 28 and won by 10 wickets. This very early finish enabled me to travel 25 miles and visit my mother in hospital, post operation. Simon Cummins was unhappy that we hadn't batted first to give my team a 'proper match' and why didn't I, as Head of Cricket, remain on site to oversee other matches that were taking place that afternoon. Perhaps he was right; perhaps I should have sought permission from him beforehand. In any case, he showed little sympathy for my family problems.

I suppose this was the lowest point of our 'relationship' although, a couple of weeks earlier, he had refused my request to take an adult from the school with me on a 300 mile round trip to Truro for a cup match. Then, on the Cricket Tour in early June, Simon suddenly decided that only Year 8 pupils were to be involved, thus seriously weakening the tour party against county opposition in Devon and Cornwall.

We won the County Shield against King's Hall – mainly due to excellent management on the day by Jo Morgan-Hughes (who was about to become the new Director of Sport) – but lost, yet again, in the JET Final, this time to Dulwich Prep by just 9 runs.

However, we were going well in the Calypso Cup and had to make the long journey to Essex to play Chigwell School in the semi-final on the last but one day of term, Thursday 1st July. Before the coach left at around 8am, Mark Brearey and Jo Morgan-Hughes took me to one side and informed me that they had got together with Simon Cummins and 'hatched a plan' which might enable me to stay on at the school. I felt excited at this turn of events. I'd told nobody outside of the school that I was due to leave, not even my mother and brother.

We won well at Chigwell, Richard Timms and Robin Lett scoring half-centuries, to qualify for another Headingley final. We arrived back at school on the stroke of midnight and I was already working on a farewell speech for the following evening . . . . . . just in case.

To date, there have been 19 Calypso/Bunbury U13 finals, but ours against Birkenhead School on Thursday 15th July must be the closest – and there have been some pretty one-sided ones. Birkenhead batted first and I have to say that our skipper had a total nightmare during their 35 over innings of 199-9. Seven bowlers were used, mostly at the wrong end or at the wrong time; Casper Bridson, who played county age-group cricket as a bowler, never bowled; the field placings were mostly incomprehensible. The Birkenhead captain, a diminutive batsman called Simon Stokes, scored 104, hitting 16 fours, mostly to the short, unpopulated third man boundary. The skipper tried one over of his usually decent leg-spin, which cost 18 runs. Crucial, as it turned out. Sitting high up in the scoring area, I felt isolated and helpless. In every National final since that day we have always had a coach, not just a manager like myself.

In our reply, we lost an early wicket before our two class batsmen – Robin Lett and Richard Timms – produced a magnificent stand of 131. Timms made 40 and Lett on 95 (4 sixes and 12 fours) was caught on the boundary by their tallest player stretching his hands above his head. A foot higher and Robin would have reached his hundred and I'm sure we would have won the game. Crucially, he had changed his bat with his score in the eighties; the original one seemed okay when I looked at it later.

Well, we got to the final over with our score 188-5 – so 12 to win, or 11 as long as we didn't lose more than another three wickets. That fateful last over went like this –

Ball 1   James Barrowman scores a single.

Ball 2   Craig Churches pulls a full toss for six. We can do it!
          Five needed off four balls. Surely . . . . .

Ball 3   Craig Churches is bowled.

35

Ball 4	Darren Clayton swings and misses.
Ball 5	Darren Clayton swings and misses.
Ball 6	Darren Clayton is bowled.

So Birkenhead won by 4 runs; utter joy for them, total despair for us. I wonder how many teams, in the history of limited overs cricket, have lost a match when batting second and their last scoring shot is a six. I'm sure we would have beaten Birkenhead nine times out of ten but, on the day, it was their day and they probably deserved it.

Well, I stayed/they kept me on and I 'worked' at the school throughout the Autumn Term for no pay. Jo Morgan-Hughes kindly gave me a personal cheque for £100 at the end of the term, which I was very pleased to pay back some years later.

In the autumn of 1998, Simon Cummins had proposed a 1st XI Cricket Tour to South Africa, planned to take place around the February half-term in 2000. Staff were to be Simon, Tim Harris and myself. I pointed out that Millfield Scholarship examinations normally took place in the week after the February half-term but Simon assured me that he had successfully put the case for these exams to be delayed until early May. I believe also that parents of Scholarship pupils were becoming increasingly irritated at having to pay full Summer Term fees, even though their son/daughter had already won a scholarship to the Senior School.

By the spring of 1999 there had been something of an uprising by influential parents – mostly mums – of girl pupils, and Simon, under some pressure, agreed that it would now be a Cricket AND Netball Tour, even though, we later discovered, netball is out of season in South Africa in February.

We had several pre-Tour meetings and David Hildreth (father of James) had been co-opted to attend. At one meeting, a female member of the games staff – can't remember who – asked what the netball girls would do while the boys were still playing cricket, the latter game being much longer of course. Quick as a flash, David replied, "Well, they could come over to the cricket and make the sandwiches for tea!" Half of us fell about; the other half didn't. Priceless.

When I was going to leave at the end of the Summer Term, Simon Cummins re-staffed the Tour, leaving me (naturally) and Tim Harris out. I don't believe that Simon was ever very keen on Tim being part of the Tour, but I simply had to accept that I wouldn't be going.

In October there was a Grand Fund Raising Dinner for the Tour, held at the Coxley Vineyard – which is now a housing estate and hopefully not built on a flood plain. I duly attended and sat next to the late and very greatly missed Simon Fuller, who was to succumb to cancer six years later. Chris Cowdrey was the Guest Speaker and he began by reminiscing how he had been in the same class at school as Simon Cummins. The wine flowed pretty freely and by the time the auction arrived I was ready to bid for almost anything. A major item was two tickets for a Manchester United Premier League game at Old Trafford later in the season and included an overnight stop at a local Holiday Inn, a guided tour around the so-called 'Theatre of Dreams' and lunch in a hospitality box. There was some lively bidding at the start before it became a head-to-head between myself and a wealthy parent (most of them have to be to afford the fees). Anyway, I managed to get it for the princely sum of £850. What would it be worth nowadays? John Etherington, who retired from Millfield Prep in 2015, successfully bid for a signed Manchester United football (£350) and, I seem to remember, got a bit of a telling off from wife Sally.

I don't think I really had any intention of going to Old Trafford myself (being a Gooner), so ended up giving away the prize to Tim Harris who had missed out on the Tour. Tim took his son Ian to United's final home game of the season in early May – against Tottenham of all teams – when they were presented with the Premier League trophy. They won the match 3-1 and pushed Arsenal into second place by a mere 18 points.

In early November, although not expecting to be part of the Tour, I was assisting in the preparation of the Tour Brochure when I had a call from David Hildreth. He, wife Judy and elder son James were booked on a separate flight to Cape Town in February and were due to return after one week of the two week tour (as James needed to be back at school at the end of the half-term break). Younger son Peter was tour skipper and four of the five matches arranged were in that first week, the second week seeing the final fixture, game reserve visits, white water rafting and so on. In an incredible act of generosity, David said he had a substantial amount of spare air miles and if I gave him just £200, I could travel to and from Cape Town with them AND spend seven nights at the Ritz Hotel there. Wow! It was a fantastic offer from David and an act of kindness and generosity I will never forget.

2000 was a big year for James Hildreth. In April, I accompanied Millfield School on their two week tour to Sri Lanka, acting as scorer. Richard Ellison led the tour party and, besides James (and David), other players included Arul Suppiah and Neil Goodman. In July, James played one of the greatest innings I've ever witnessed – from anyone, anywhere. Batting at No.1 for the West against the Midlands in the Bunbury Festival, on not a great pitch, he was run out on the last ball of the 50 over innings for a magnificent 151 – made out of 207-8. In August he was opening for England in the U15 World Cup with a certain Alastair Cook. So, as I said, quite a year. James has now completed 13 seasons in the Somerset team and what a fantastic 2015 he had with the highest run aggregate (1620) in Division 1.

I enjoyed my half-tour experience in South Africa and have to say that Simon Cummins seemed genuinely pleased that I'd made it out there, inviting me to manage the team in the four fixtures. We won three of these games, the last victory being on the middle Sunday at Langa township, just outside Cape Town. David, Judy, James and myself then set off for the airport for the overnight flight home, calling in at Stellenbosch en route. The fifth and final match was won, when we were back in the UK, making it four wins out of five. It must be said, however, that we were playing prep school opposition who were at their weakest as their school year starts on 1st January – which I've long thought ours should in the UK, though nobody ever seems to agree with me. The only reason the academic year starts in September is because, goodness knows how many years ago, schoolchildren were required to help gather in the harvest – potato picking and so on. I don't think that applies nowadays. Surely it would be better if public examinations were sat in late October/early November, rather than in May and June. I'm sure the hay fever sufferers would agree with me. I also think there should be just one examining board, but I'm now drifting away from my sporting life . . . . .

There was certainly a noticeable difference in the standard of prep school opposition when we undertook our second South African Tour in December 2002, failing to win any of the five matches played.

For the 2000, two week tour, pupils had to pay £600 each, a sum which I couldn't believe would be enough, particularly as the cost of including half a dozen staff had to be taken into consideration. So it proved and I'm led to believe that there was a considerable financial loss. Pupils on the tour stayed in hotels or were hosted by opposition families. I'm sure that hosting on these tours will become a thing of the past, what with CRB/DBS issues.

On Maundy Thursday 2000, every Millfield employee received a letter saying that Simon Cummins was taking a sabbatical during the Summer Term and would officially 'leave office' on 31st August. Although we had our well-documented ups and downs, there were a number of very positive aspects of his eleven terms as Headmaster. In August he sent me a treasured hand-written letter – his last as Head, as he said – congratulating me on the 1st XI winning the Calypso Cup in July. A couple of years later I was at Lord's for a Dinner when I met him again and he greeted me with a warm embrace. Now working for Odgers Ray & Berndtson, the head-hunting organisation, he told me that he had just chaired a meeting to appoint a new CEO for Middlesex County Cricket Club. I think Angus Fraser got the job.

CHAPTER 10
New Beginnings

While I continued as Head of Cricket, Mark Brearey became the first-ever 1st XI coach, for three years, until he moved to Hampshire in September 2002 to be Deputy Head at Forres Sandle Manor Prep School. Mark, who I once saw score 146* in a 'last 16' National Village cup match for Butleigh, proved an excellent, hardworking coach and certainly began well when we made up for the previous year's disappointment by winning the Calypso Cup for the second time in four years. We had an excellent team in 2000, including four top players from the previous year in Lett, Parry, Barrowman and Santa-Olalla. We also had an outstanding opening batsman in Liam Lewis, who later in the year moved on to Blundell's, was 1st XI captain there in 2004-2005 and has since been a successful opening bat for Devon in their Minor Counties team.

Instead of going down to Devon and Cornwall for the post exams Cricket Tour, we decided on pastures new for just one year and ventured towards London, playing matches against Bishop Stortford College, Hertfordshire U13s (both won) and Essex U13s (lost). The Essex opener, Ollie Allen (son of footballer Clive), scored 101, while none of the other twenty-one batsmen in the match got past 20. Incidentally, Ollie Allen's opening partner that day was the 2015 Warwickshire captain, Varun Chopra (caught behind for 2). We concluded the tour on the Monday by spending the day at Chessington World of Adventures; my recollection is that it was a truly frightening day on some of those rides, though, as we came away, the players insisted that I'd avoided the REALLY scary ones.

The one disappointment that season was the loss in the JET final to Whitgift by just 5 runs, but we did gain revenge just eight days later when we defeated them at home in the Calypso semi-final by 42 runs. Half an hour after this win, we had torrential rain of such intensity that the entire square was quickly under water. If it had arrived an hour earlier and caused the match to be abandoned we would have lost on run rate. We also won the County Shield, narrowly defeating Taunton state school Castle by just 9 runs at the County Ground in Taunton. We (not me) gave the impression that we thought our 25 over score of 174-3 to be impregnable – but it very nearly wasn't.

So, it was off to Headingley for our third final there in four years where we were to face Nottingham High School on Thursday 13th July. I drove the team up to Leeds on my own (we were meeting up with Mark Brearey at a service station on the M1) when, lo and behold, we broke down, just before crossing the Avonmouth Bridge. Overhead cameras picked up our plight and the motorway police arrived in minutes, informing me that we had broken down at one of the busiest motorway locations in Western Europe. Pete Cabble arrived from Foundry Garage – we'd become firm friends – with a replacement vehicle and we weren't too long delayed.

After an overnight stay in a hotel to the north of Leeds, we set off for the ground in our minibus, only to lose our way and get lost! In our slight defence, of all the Test grounds, Headingley is by far the most difficult to find, certainly when compared to Lord's, the Oval, Trent Bridge, Edgbaston and Old Trafford, which are all on main routes. At one point, we stopped and asked someone the way to Headingley and they replied they'd never heard of it! Anyway, we eventually arrived about forty minutes before the start, leaving little time for the usual pre-match preparations but plenty of looks from ESCA officials.

We batted first and were wobbling somewhat at 49-3 before an excellent stand of 101 between Liam Lewis (81) and James Barrowman (41*) was key to a final total of 167-4. We worked steadily through their batting line-up, Robin Lett taking 4-20, before bowling them out for 113 in the final over; this after being 98-4. I have to say that Nottingham had the nastiest and most hostile parents I've ever come across – and there have been a few of those – making it clear that this was a match between the haves and the have nots and that Millfield won national competitions

Myself, Gavin Hamilton and Mark Brearey
Calypso Final Winners, 2000

only by buying in top international superstars. Liam Lewis and I had a chuckle about this afterwards, when thinking of the hours we had spent on cold winter mornings (7am starts), with me firing down balls at him from the bowling machine. At one stage in the Nottingham innings, one of their batsmen was given run out when 'keeper Harry had removed the bails without the ball in his gloves. Mark Brearey ran onto the pitch to get the decision successfully reversed. However, this did little to 'placate' the Nottingham parents who, I reckon, merely thought that Mark was being patronising.

1st XI skipper in 2001 was Max Waller, who the year before had wisely changed from medium pace bowling to leg-spin. Max had been a boarder from a very young age – his father Ian being in the Army – and from Year 6, when he was just ten, I used to take him down to Taunton on a Friday evening for Somerset coaching, followed, of course, by McDonald's on the way back to school (and probably the odd sherbet lemon as well). Whenever I meet up with former pupils, they almost invariably begin by asking if I still give out sherbet lemons.

"I'm afraid not; they were banned."

"Shame!"

"Health and Safety has a lot to answer for."

Or it may have been for some other reason.

This was the first question Ben Duckett asked me when I congratulated him after he had scored 144 not out for Northamptonshire v Somerset in September 2014.

Besides being 1st XI coach, Mark Brearey and his wife Yvonne were also houseparents at Edgarley House. They had two young boys – Ben and Henry – and in late April, Ellie arrived on the scene. On the first Saturday in May we had to travel to Ryde on the Isle of Wight to play an early round of the JET Shield. We would be away all day, travelling by minibus and then car ferry from Southampton. When I explained to Mark that this was simply the only date we could play the match – less than two weeks after Ellie's birth – his only response was, "Will you tell the wife or shall I?"

We won very comfortably, but went out in the next round to one of the best Cheltenham College Junior School teams of recent times. However, although lacking the all-round talent of recent teams and helped in no small measure by Max Waller's 51 wickets, we did incredibly well to reach yet another Calypso Final at Headingley. Our opponents were Birchfield from the Midlands who had one of those 'once in a lifetime' teams – not heard of before and not since. Put into bat, we struggled just past the 100 and they easily knocked off the runs for the loss of just one wicket (a run out). Our No.6 batsman, a delightful Indian boy by the name of Pratyush Bose, had travelled all the way from New Delhi to play in the match, only to be run out without facing a ball. I have to say he took it very well; he wasn't a bowler either.

Incidentally, of the 19 Calypso/Bunbury U13 National finals, Whitgift have won eight, Millfield Prep six and the other five by that number of different schools once.

In September of that year, 2001, I received a letter from a gentleman called Alun Jenkins. Alun and his lovely wife Elaine had two sons, Ross and William, and lived in the small village of Priddy, up in the Mendip Hills. A few years earlier, while on a family holiday in Cornwall, Alun had dived into the sea and hit his head on an unseen rock below the surface of the water. Elaine managed to drag him out of the water before being airlifted to Treliske Hospital in Truro and thence to Odstock Hospital in Salisbury for rehab. Alun was paralysed from the waist down – 'relieved' it wasn't from the neck down – and destined to spend the rest of his life in a wheelchair. He was now writing to me in the hope of getting Ross into Millfield Prep from his tiny primary school at Priddy. Ross had been selected for the Somerset U11 team a year young that summer and Alun enclosed a video of him opening the batting in a couple of county games. I went to see the school's new Headmaster, Kevin Cheney, and suggested inviting Ross for an interview to assess his potential. I also urged Kevin to negotiate with the bursar to try and agree a financial package, stressing that, surely, 'this is what Millfield is all about'.

Well, I believe Kevin did give Alun and Elaine a good financial deal and Ross started at Millfield Prep in January 2002, before William, three years younger, entered Year 4 in the September. Ross was an outstanding cricketer who even played the occasional 1st XI match in Year 6 before two full seasons in the team in 2003 and 2004. His crowning glory was a superb, unbeaten century to win the 2004 JET Final at Oxford when all had seemed lost. Ross was a talented all-round sportsman, though I always considered that rugby and hockey failed to get the most/best out of him during his time at the school.

William – usually referred to as Will – was of the same ilk as his older brother; a gifted rugby and hockey player as well as being an outstanding wicketkeeper/ batsman. As a 'keeper, he stood up to almost everything and brought off some miraculous stumpings, none better than in the last over of the 2006 JET final, when Daniel Lewis-Williams achieved a hat-trick and we won an improbable victory by 2 runs. Ironically, Will gave up wicketkeeping in his mid-teens - perhaps because he grew very tall – and is now a fast bowling all-rounder with Bath in the West of England Premier League.

After Alun's accident, the family moved from Priddy into a converted cottage in North Wootton. They were kind enough to put me up – or was it put up with me? – for a week after a hernia operation. I also spent Christmas Day with them in 2004, the year my mother had passed away in July. For some years Alun was an excellent Chairman of the Somerset Cricket Board Youth Committee, responsible for age-group and District cricket. A first-rate structure was devised and set-up under Alun's stewardship and is still very much in operation today.

Jo Morgan-Hughes should take all the credit for getting the 2002 captain, James Fear, into Millfield Prep. In the summer of 1999, Jo took an U11 team to play at Wells Central School where James was the star player, scoring runs and taking wickets. By good 'fortune', James's father Mike was off work with a broken arm and was umpiring the match. So one thing led to another and James started at Millfield Prep that September – much to the annoyance, I always felt, of Central's Headteacher Mike King. He wasn't very happy to lose his star player and even less so when Bradley Derrick and the Barrowman boys – James and Alasdair – followed suit. In a similar way, Division 2 teams in the County Championship must be unhappy when they lose star players to the big boys in Division 1; David Willey from Northamptonshire to Yorkshire being a good example.

Matt Perry, James Fear and myself
School Open Day, 2002

We hadn't qualified for the Calypso Cup in 2002, but played some good cricket, James Fear leading from the front and scoring over 800 runs. However, this was to be Mark Brearey's third and final year as 1st XI coach as he was moving on to pastures new. I surprised –and probably upset – a few people by nominating Simon Wynn to take over as 1st team coach from 2003. I suspected that Simon might relish the opportunity to look after such a team; for some years he had coached the U12A rugby and hockey teams but would now be eager to take on the 'top job' in a major sport. I also thought that we would go well together, particularly as he was a disciplinarian and I was looked on as a bit of a softee (or was it soft touch?), somewhat falling short where discipline was concerned.

During the summer of 1999, when I was due to be leaving, David Beal – who had been my Somerset Schools' U13 captain in 1979 – was appointed as a coach in the Cricket Department as from 1st September. Dave had played a few games for Somerset in the early nineties, still holds the all-time bowling record (over 900 wickets) in the old Somerset League and I reckon was looking for something of a career change or a new challenge. Dave also assisted on the grounds in his early years at the school, before becoming full time in the Games Department. Dave has a Level 3 coaching qualification, which has enabled him to become a highly thought of and indeed sought after coach, both singly and in groups. His infectious enthusiasm for the game is there for all to see. Besides cricket, Dave has also been much involved in running hockey teams (boys and girls) – he got himself a qualification in that sport too – as well as teams in my annual Football Tournaments. If as a pupil you have Dave (unfortunately a Manchester United fan, but nobody's perfect) in charge of your multi-activity on a Wednesday or Saturday afternoon, you would know, whatever it was, that he would put 100% into running it – not always the case elsewhere. I will always contend that if I hadn't been on the point of leaving in 1999 Dave would never have come to Millfield Prep. His appointment has proved an inspirational one in every respect.

Mention of Dave's stint on the grounds leads me, quite rightly, to talk about the Grounds and Gardens Department at Millfield Preparatory School. They can be summed up in just one word – superb. I've lost count of the number of times I've welcomed sports teams – mainly cricket, of course - to the school over the years and the first thing staff and parents mention are the grounds and gardens. Pitches beautifully prepared, marked and set out to perfection, the grass manicured to a perfect length and thickness. Bob Dutton left school at the age of 15 at Easter in 1969 (you could do so then), when Harold Wilson was Prime Minister, so has achieved an almost unbelievable 47 years in Millfield's employment, most of them at the helm at the Prep School. Acker (Leeds 'til I die), Graham and Dean are his principal staff while Colin has completed thousands of hours of conscientious and dedicated work on the gardens. I salute them all, more especially as they are hardly paid a king's ransom. If you couldn't enjoy coaching and running teams at

Millfield Prep in these fantastic conditions, you ought to seriously consider doing something else.

On the subject of groundsmen, I must mention the following gentlemen – Gerry Wilson, for over forty years Cricket Coach and Head of Grounds at Millfield School (the 'new' 1st XI Cricket Pavilion – built in 2005 – is named after him); Dennis Breakwell, now (mostly) retired as Head Groundsman at King's College in Taunton, who must have prepared thousands of superb wickets for over twenty years, particularly during the six weeks of County Festivals in July and August; Adie Davis, Head Groundsman for many years at King's School, Bruton; Craig Keast, Head Groundsman at Wells Cathedral School for over twenty-seven years and a proud Cornishman who bowled leg-breaks with much success for Cornwall U15s in 1980. Finally, I go back to my first teaching post at Uphill Secondary School where 'Nick' Nicholson spent so many hours tending the cricket square. I salute them all.

Within three months of taking over as 1st XI coach, Simon Wynn – together with Dave Beal and myself – were taking sixteen players on an 11 day tour to the Cape Town area of South Africa in December 2002. We played five matches, drawing two and losing three; a poor record, you may say, but we were not as strong as usual, hadn't qualified for the following season's Calypso Cup and, with sixteen players to keep happy, were never able to field our strongest team in any one match. We played mainly club sides, since schools had broken up for Christmas, and also the traditional visit to play a township side (again it was Langa). Our captain and best player, Matthew Spelman, even had to leave after the third match as he had a pre-booked Christmas holiday in America. I did hear from an informed source that the club opposition had strengthened their teams by borrowing a star player or two from a neighbouring club when they were told it was Millfield they would be playing. I greeted this news with a mixture of amusement and annoyance. People always seem to assume that every Millfield team, in whatever sport, at whatever age and at whatever level – A, B, C or D – is going to be brilliant. This is not always the case and, more often than not, isn't the case at all. Anyway, it was a most enjoyable experience and Simon and Dave were excellent in all they did to ensure things ran smoothly. We stayed throughout at the Breakwater Lodge Hotel (no hosting on my tours), just off the Waterfront, which used to be the main prison in the area but has now been very tastefully converted. It was an ideal base, the rooms were clean and comfortable and the choice at breakfast wide-ranging enough to suit most tastes. We did all the usual trips, such as Robben Island (I comfortably survived the boat rides there and back) and Table Mountain, though, for some reason, didn't visit Newlands. This still irks Dave Beal to this day!

During Simon's early years coaching and looking after the team we worked pretty well together but there were inevitably one or two disagreements over selection/policy, etc. However, as time went on, I became more and more agreeable for Simon to take full control of the playing side while I concentrated on administration and match day scoring.

In 1992, my first year in charge of the 1st XI, we played 28 matches and I used only 14 players – and the batting order rarely changed. By the early 2000s I realised/was told (!) that this state of affairs could no longer happen. Another factor was that, when I started, very few, if any, parents came to watch; by the turn of the century this was all changing. Parents were hovering around the pavilion or prowling around the boundary; so if a boarder's parent had driven 150 miles to watch his son play, he would, often unrealistically, expect him to bowl eight overs and bat in the top four. Simon has become an expert in selection/winning/ bringing players into the game, all in one go. Not easy. I would never have coped with this; nor would I have coped with my accomplished opening batsman, having played well in the first six matches of the season, being told – probably against his and his parents' wishes – that he would have to miss the next game to throw a javelin at Yeovil or wherever in an athletics event.

Of all the major sports, cricket is by far the most difficult to run – by a country mile. It takes much longer than rugby and hockey, is at the 'fag' end of the school year, while one always suspected that many of the cricket staff prayed for rain on a Wednesday and Saturday, so they could mark exam papers, do reports or even take the wife shopping at Waitrose. However, I am sure they will all verify that I always thanked them for their efforts at the end of term. Sincerely meant because, as I always said, I couldn't operate a 13 team department without them. However, it has to be said that during my time at Millfield Prep, cricket has always suffered somewhat due to a significant lack of coaching depth and expertise in its structure – certainly well below that enjoyed by rugby and hockey.

However, I must pay tribute to the late Kevin Jackson. Kevin was a music teacher at the school, enthusiastically coached the U12B cricket and hockey teams and was a charming and kindly staffroom colleague. After a battle with cancer, Kevin very sadly passed away in November 2004 when only in his late forties. The following year I set up the Kevin Jackson Memorial Award and, since 2005, a trophy has been awarded to the boy or girl in Year 7 who has participated in cricket and/or hockey for the school and who has also been active in the Music Department (see picture, right). A prestigious annual award to remember a much loved and greatly missed gentleman.

In 2003, although we hadn't qualified for the Calypso Cup – now in its last year – we did get to the JET final, having won the semi-final against a St. Olave's team with a certain Jonny Bairstow in their ranks. However, in the final, we came

John Hall with the
Kevin Jackson Memorial Award, 2009

up against a brilliant schoolboy player in Sam Northeast, now captain of Kent. He was on 94 when extremely well caught by Jack Waller (who was to be captain the following year) on the square-leg boundary; a couple of feet higher and it would have been a six and Sam's hundred. Sam is a delightful young man, always willing to stop and chat; he is very unlucky not to have received any England recognition at present, not even for the Lions or 'A' team. His 132 for Kent against Somerset at Taunton in 2014 was quite superb.

2004 saw the Calypso sponsorship end and be taken up by the lengendary David English and called the Bunbury Cup. Our quarter-final against Yateley Manor was delayed and delayed – mainly because they were away camping in the penultimate week of term (which we now do), culminating in the match being played on the Friday afternoon. We beat them by 10 wickets, which was hardly surprising as most of their players struggled to stay awake after four nights under canvas and very little sleep. Then came the pantomime – in late June. Semi-final opponents were King's College Junior School, Wimbledon at home (thankfully) and the only day they reluctantly agreed to play was the following Thursday, our penultimate day of term and the deadline date for the tie to be played.

King's arrived in high dudgeon, in parents' cars (never a good idea) and the weather was uncertain with rain never far away. We tried to start on our main square; they refused the offer to play on either of our excellent astroturf pitches, so hasty arrangements were made to play on the 1st XI square at Millfield Senior School, four miles away. We agreed on a 25 overs a side match, lost the toss, were inevitably inserted . . . and it rained again. What was most annoying was that, while the rains fell on the two cricket grounds that day, we could see that the sun was shining for most of the time on the surrounding hills. King's again refused to

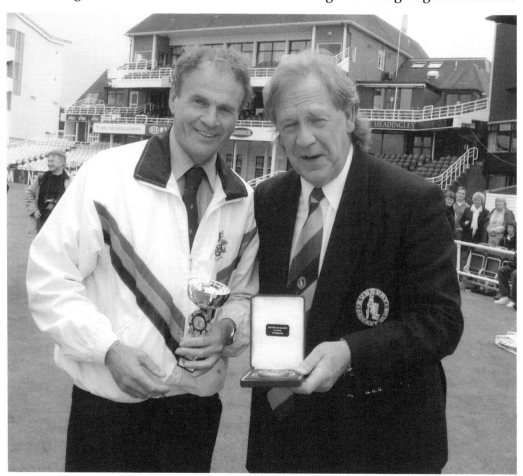

Receiving the Winning Manager's Award from David English, Headingley 2004

play on an artificial pitch at Millfield, turned down the choice of a bowl-off and set off home without any agreement on either side as to what was going to happen next.

Well, the ESCA organisers ruled that a toss of the coin would take place at 11am the following morning – Millfield Prep's Open Day – and ESCA's Dennis Houghton called me on my mobile when I was out in the middle umpiring an exhibition match. I called heads and Dennis said the coin he had tossed (faraway at Kendal in the Lake District) had come up heads so we would be going to another Headingley final. Mel Chalke, mum of our diminutive wicketkeeper George, ran on to the pitch, gave me a hug and a kiss and handed me a glass of champagne! King's were furious that they hadn't been involved in the toss – which would have been quite difficult – and one of their parents, a barrister or maybe just a barrack room lawyer, threatened everything under the sun, but nothing came of it.

As previously mentioned, we had already won the JET Shield earlier in the week (thanks to Ross Jenkins's unbeaten hundred) and now we were to play a Staffordshire Middle School in the last-ever Headingley final. Christchurch Middle School had overcome a couple of independent schools to reach the final, including the notable scalp of Manchester Grammar in the semi-final. We stayed at a classy hotel just up the road from Headingley, so we wouldn't be in any danger of getting lost this year. Simon Wynn arrived just in time for breakfast at the hotel, having been at Jo Morgan-Hughes' wedding the day before. We really had to put Christchurch into bat – the weather was uncertain – but the whole occasion was a bit too much for them. They were all out for just 49 and our openers knocked off the runs in the eighth over on the stroke of lunch.

On Saturday 5th September 2015, I was delighted to attend George Chalke's wedding when he married the lovely Georgie at Boconnoc in Cornwall. The Morgan-Hughes family, Dave Beal and the newly married Chris Chapman and his wife were also there and it was a pleasure to be part of such a happy occasion. I will always remember Mel Chalke for the wonderful fundraising she did a few years ago to bring a township rugby team from South Africa over to England for a tour. With Mel at the helm, various functions were arranged – Dinners, auctions and so on with the result that around £30,000 was raised. So everything was paid for and the players and officials of the township team had only to bring some spending money and very little else. I know it will be said that many Millfield parents are very well off and can afford to be generous, but someone has to actually make things like this happen. Mel and her 'committee' certainly did. That township rugby team had the experience of a lifetime; three weeks they will remember for ever. Mel, I will forever salute you!

2005 and more controversy! We arrived at the last week of term with a major fixture problem. We were due to visit Whitgift in Surrey for the Bunbury semi-final, but when could we fit it in? It had to be played that week. We were in the County Shield final on the Monday, then up to Oxford for the JET finals on the Tuesday; the Wednesday was really a non-starter as the Year 8 players would miss out on their social event of the year, the Leavers' Prom; Thursday, Whitgift couldn't do and Friday was Open Day (now Speech Day & Prizegiving) and the school's last day of term.

I discussed the problem over the phone from my office – goodness knows how many hours I spent in there over the years – with Simon Wynn and we reluctantly agreed that there was no other solution but to withdraw from the competition. I called Duncan White at Whitgift to explain the situation and relay to him our decision. He was surprised, almost disappointed, but appreciated my early call.

Well, on the Monday morning the proverbial you know what hit the fan, the Director of Sport wasn't happy (why hadn't he been consulted?) and then the two Headmasters got involved. After much – mostly heated – discussion on the Monday and early Tuesday, it was decided that our decision to withdraw would be rescinded (I was outvoted) and that Dave Beal and Richard Allen (the latter on the understanding that his son would be in the team) would take the side up to Whitgift early on the Wednesday morning for a 10am start. This would hopefully enable the team to be back in time for the evening Prom.

I did get my way on one matter and this was by insisting that star batsman Daniel Bell-Drummond from Year 7 stayed behind to play in the U12 County Final at Frome that afternoon. I wanted us to have the best chance of qualifying for the following year's Bunbury Cup and Daniel was obviously a key player. Queen's College were our opponents in that U12 final and Daniel's magnificent 127 not out (still a record in the competition) ensured a comfortable win and qualification for 2006. Vital, as you will shortly find out. As for the match at Whitgift, we lost the toss, were put into bat, were bowled out cheaply, lost by 7 wickets and the players were back in good time for the Prom – and the opportunity to get to know the love of their life even better. Captain in this somewhat traumatic season was Nick Pang, who deserves great credit for the way he handled things both on and off the field. He also batted and bowled well and set a great example in the field.

As you may have guessed, 1st XI skipper in 2006 was Daniel Bell-Drummond. The remarkable win in the JET final has already been mentioned; defending a meagre total of 118 against St. Olave's from York, we triumphed by just 2 runs. However, I will always insist that our success in the Bunbury Cup a couple of weeks later was even more remarkable. We travelled up to Northamptonshire for the final at the new venue of Oundle School, enjoyed a very pleasant evening meal at the nearby Talbot Hotel before settling down for the night at a boarding house in the school. As usual, the weather was uncertain the following morning, but we had more than the weather to worry about when vice-captain Will Heywood had to drop up through illness half an hour before the start. Our opponents in the final were Loughborough Grammar School who, unusually where any Millfield team is involved, were hot favourites to win. They had lost in the 2005 final to Whitgift and were very determined to succeed this year.

We won the toss, put them in and their openers set off like the proverbial train, punishing some wayward deliveries from our opening bowlers. In fact, they had reached 96 in only eleven overs when Shiv Thakor (now Derbyshire 1st XI) lofted the ball into the long-off area, perfectly safely he thought, only to see Charlie Hartley sprint round the boundary and dive full length to take a marvellous catch. Until that moment, Loughborough looked set for a total in excess of 300, but Charlie's catch that day changed the whole 'feel' of that final. We had already lost Max Palmer-Jeffrey to a broken arm when he had collided with Charlie early in the match when going for the same ball. Loughborough very kindly lent us their 12th Man to field for the rest of our innings.

We set out to try and surpass their total of 224-6 (35 overs), opening with Daniel Bell-Drummond (who was on 996 runs for the season) and the 2007 captain in waiting, Henry Hayes. We started well, DB-D made a composed 54, everyone chipped in and, with ten balls to spare, Daniel Lewis-Williams pulled a six over mid-wicket to win the most famous of victories by 4 wickets (in reality, 3 wickets, as we had only ten batsmen after the earlier disasters with Will and Max).

Loughborough's players, staff and parents were the most sporting of opposition schools you could wish to meet. Whilst obviously disappointed at the result, they warmly congratulated us on our success and I was delighted when they finally won the Bunbury Cup the following year, defeating Brentwood School in the final. David English conducted the presentation of awards in that inimitable way of his and I was disappointed that, as was the norm on these National cricket occasions, there was nobody from Millfield Prep's senior management team present on the day.

So Daniel Bell-Drummond reached 1,050 1st XI runs for the season, which is still a record, despite Cameron Steel (1,036 in 2009) and Will Smeed (1,027 in 2015) coming close. Charlie Hartley is still the fastest bowler in my 22 seasons managing the 1st XI – he checks that this is the case whenever we are in contact. He is currently on the Kent staff. I know he won't mind my recalling the fact that when he arrived at Millfield Prep as a first-time boarder in September 2005 at the age of 11 he was very homesick in the first week or so and we were concerned he might run off and try and get back home to Worcester. So, on the first Wednesday of term, I took him and a friend (also homesick) to watch a couple of hours of Somerset cricket in Taunton, followed, naturally enough, by a visit to McDonald's. I like to think it helped and Charlie was certainly a tower of strength in the 1st XI for two seasons.

One of the key members of our side that year was Matthew Hobden and in the Loughborough final he took 2-24 and scored 34 valuable runs. The whole cricket world was shocked and saddened early in 2016 with the news that he had died following a tragic accident in Scotland. Matt was just 22 years old, was on the Sussex staff and a bright future was predicted – mainly as a fast bowler but also as a more than useful batsman. The England team wore black armbands on the second day of the Test match in Cape Town.

A truly tragic loss, especially in one so young.

Matthew Hobden standing to my left
as part of the 1st XI Cricket Team in 2006
Winners of the National David English / Bunbury Cup and the National J.E.T. Shield

CHAPTER 11

The Final Years

In 2007, under the astute leadership of Henry Hayes, who had been awarded a scholarship at Eton College for that September, we played attractive, attacking cricket but, perhaps surprisingly, failed to win either of the National titles. We had an off day at Oxford in the JET Shield final and lost out to a strong Brentwood School side in the Bunbury Cup semi-final after a long drive to Essex on the morning of the game. Put into bat, we were 49-1 before subsiding to 57-4. After that mini collapse it was always going to be an uphill struggle.

2008 skipper Charlie Vickery had arrived at the school as an 8 year-old, after playing in my 'rebel' Somerset U10 team there, and convincing him and his parents, Mark and Julie, that Millfield Prep was the school for him – certainly where cricket was concerned. Charlie wasn't the first to have followed this path during my 23 years at the school and wouldn't be the last. His two best mates in the team were wicketkeeper Alex Gould and all-rounder Tom Brock, both of whom would be at Oxbridge five years later. We were again drawn to play Brentwood School in the semi-final of the Bunbury Cup – and, for some strange reason, away again – with a similar result to 2007. Cameron Steel, still an U12, top-scored with an excellent fifty – a very encouraging innings with the following season in mind, against an excellent Brentwood attack of real pace and high class spin.

Another memory of this year was when the block fixture with Taunton Prep on a Saturday in May 'clashed' with a Grand Charity Ball in the sports hall. I stayed behind at school to assist with taking trays of sandwiches and cakes to the out grounds as the dining hall was out of action. I have to say that I was beginning to think that the Ball was a bit of a nuisance until I later heard that it had raised around £20,000 for Children's Hospice South West. A fantastic effort for a truly worthy cause. By the way, the 1st XI was bowled out for 41 at Taunton, chief destroyer being future England Women's player Jodie Dibble.

This year saw the school winning the National 8-a-Side U11 Hardball Competition for the fourth time. Since first entering in 1995, we had enjoyed a thoroughly decent record. Although it's a pairs game, it IS 'proper' cricket and entails first a county, then a regional competition, ending up with finals day, involving the eight regional winners. We were runners-up in both 1995 (Headingley) and 1996 (Edgbaston) before finally triumphing at Edgbaston in 1998, under the captaincy of Nick Page. Nick and younger sister Sarah both went on to become international hockey players.

Nine years after this success I received a Saturday night 'phone call from star batsman Robin Lett, urging me to drive over to David Nuttall's palatial residence

HSA Healthcare Champions, Edgbaston 1998

at West Huntspill, where most of that winning team were gathered, mainly, I seem to remember, to celebrate David's parents' wedding anniversary. So I dutifully got the car out and travelled over from Wells (in heavy rain) and there they all were (now aged about 20) in in their dinner jackets and with their incredibly attractive girlfriends. I have a treasured framing to record the event.

The following year, finals day had moved to Old Trafford, where we lost in the final by just 7 runs. Skipper Max Waller was bowled off the final ball, a picture of this moment, with bails flying, appearing in the following day's Telegraph Sport. Two years later we were back at Old Trafford and, with some excellent batting and skipper Matt Spelman's luck with the toss in every match, we were victorious against Yorkshire opponents Malsis.

In 2005, after ten years of running the team on my own, I decided to involve Dave Beal (who ran the U11A team in the Saturday and Wednesday matches) so that he was coach and I was manager/administrator. We proved to be the ideal partnership and that year, with an admittedly strong side, won the National title at Oundle School, defeating Parkfield School from Surrey in the final. Henry Hayes was captain and a key member of the side was 10 year-old Ben Duckett.

Our success in 2008, again at Oundle School and with John Hall as captain, saw us playing some exceptional U11 cricket and we looked forward to an outstanding 1st XI in 2010.

The 2009 season was nothing if not interesting. We were knocked out of the JET Shield by St John's-on-the-Hill in the first week in May – reckoned to be the earliest elimination ever – resulting in two parents (both male) squaring up to each other, each blaming the other's offspring for the defeat! We hadn't qualified for the Bunbury Cup but did gain a hugely satisfying win in the first ever National T20 Competition for prep schools. In all the matches, Cameron Steel (now on the Middlesex staff) and Year 7 star Max O'Leary (now a Bristol City goalkeeper) regularly gave us a good start with 50+ on the board within five overs. We defeated Bedford School in a tense semi-final before beating Colet Court from London in a well contested final on the superbly appointed ground at Wormsley Park in Buckinghamshire (owned by the Getty family). It turned out that this competition was a complete one-off; it hasn't happened since, mainly, I gather, because nobody could be found to run it. The boys enjoyed wearing the smart, navy coloured clothing from Woodworm, also worn three years later by the girls' team in their National exploits. Mirage Interiors have also been very welcome 1st XI shirt sponsors. Cameron Steel led from the front with his batting (1,036 runs) and effective spin bowling. In the match against Mid-Glamorgan, he and Daniel Escott put on an unbeaten 263 for the 2nd wicket, both scoring hundreds.

Andy Tait led the team in 2010, which certainly upset Daniel Escott (or more probably his father, who withdrew him from the school at half-term when he had already scored over 600 runs and taken 24 wickets with his leg-spin). Daniel - a delightful, well-mannered and extremely bright young man - had already won a scholarship to Winchester College (where he was to spend five highly successful years in the 1st XI) and I was very disappointed with his father's action. I had persuaded him to send Daniel to Millfield Prep for Years 7 and 8, recognising him as an outstanding prospect whenever I saw him perform for the Devon age-group teams. To be honest, though, we hardly missed him as we had real strength in depth that year. In all, we played 25 matches, winning 20 and drawing the other five, the season ending on a high note with a 6 wicket win against St. Olave's in the final of the JET Shield. Almost incredibly, we had again failed to qualify for the Bunbury Cup, losing to Taunton Prep on their ground the previous June. This year, we played that same Taunton team three times and won very easily on each occasion . . . . .

2011 skipper was Archie Dunning and he led the team to a thoroughly decent record of 19 wins in 24 matches, with only three defeats. We reached the last four of the JET Shield, but went out to Whitgift in the Bunbury Cup semi-final. In the U11 Hardball, we reached the finals at Repton School, finishing a very creditable

Oran McNulty, 2011 Season

third. In the County Final that year against King's Hall, I was relaying the success of Oran McNulty (4 wickets for 2 runs) to his mum Clare back at school, who was waiting to collect her younger son Finn.

Captain in 2012 was Teddie Casterton who had been a regular opener in the 1st XI when in Year 7. In a wet summer, Teddie was a real mainstay of the batting, scoring a fine hundred at Colston's in June – which I missed as I had to take the U13 Girls to a tournament at King's School Bruton (which they won). I had also seen Teddie score an excellent century for Somerset U12s against Essex the previous August. In the Bunbury Cup we went out to a state middle school, St. Michael's from Dorset, in Round 1 by just four runs, in a match played on the U11 artificial pitch. We reckoned it was probably a blessing in disguise as we were very unlikely to make much further progress in the competition. Fitting in extra matches would also have been a real problem. We again finished third nationally in the U11 Hardball Competition, the new permanent venue now being Oakham School.

In my 23rd and final year at Millfield Prep the 1st XI captain was Ned Dunning, younger brother of Archie and twin of Lottie (Head Girl in the Summer Term). We went out of the JET Shield before half-term, losing to old rivals King's Hall by 5 wickets. At one stage we were 42-8, but did make a recovery of sorts to reach 104, Jordan Wood at No.10 top scoring with an unbeaten 38. At the end of term, Jordan was the fifteenth and final winner of the Chris Twort Merit Award. Jordan was my best-ever left-back in 21 years running the school U11 football team. In the autumn of 2015 I was pleased to be able to take Jordan to ISFA U16 trials in London and Shrewsbury and was really delighted when he was selected for the ISFA National side. Back to cricket and we did gain revenge against King's Hall when we defeated them by 10 wickets in the County Shield Final. Will Smeed (only in

Year 6) scored an unbeaten 52, he and Ned taking us to victory with five overs to spare. In a repeat of 2011 we went out to Whitgift in the Bunbury Cup semi-final, but only by 30 runs. Their prolific opening batsmen put on 104 for the first wicket; however, the week before in a mini block fixture, that same opening pair had put on an unbroken 242 in just 30 overs for the first wicket, both scoring hundreds. I was working overtime in the scorebox that day. On adjoining pitches, however, our U11 and U12 teams both defeated Whitgift – a very encouraging two results

Jordan Wood, 2013 Season

for future prospects. As you may imagine, Whitgift went on to complete a hat-trick of Bunbury Cup successes (under the genial David Ward), but we could sense that our time would now come.

During this, my penultimate term at the school, I survived – just – a Disciplinary Hearing (sensitively chaired by Mark Suddaby, the Bursar), the principal charge against me being that I took three hungry boarders to McDonald's on Wednesday 1st May in an 'unauthorised vehicle' (my car) after arriving back from cricket at Monkton Combe to find no packed suppers had been left. However, a few days later, worse was to follow when I was sacked as manager of the U11 Hardball team, a role I had faithfully and conscientiously carried out from the year I first entered the school in the competition in 1995. In January, Dave Beal had become Director of Cricket Coaching and the newly arrived Marc Gardiner (Head of Games) was to take over from Dave as U11A coach. The decision to remove me from office as Hardball manager was a clear reversal of what was agreed at a cricket meeting in November 2012. What made it worse was that we were nailed-on certainties to qualify at county and then regional level and hot favourites to become National champions. This duly happened and we won the four matches at Oakham School by huge margins to win the competition for a fifth time. We were so strong that we were able to field a team of eight county players. Although Dave Beal made all the cricket decisions, I had been cruelly denied the right to be with him for our third national success together and my fifth in all. I'd even already bought and paid for the green caps the players traditionally wore in this competition.

On Tuesday 24th September 2013 I decided it was time to go, informed the Headmistress by e-mail at 7.27 that morning and left at the end of term. The following June I was invited to the school's Speech Day & Prizegiving. I replied that I regretted I was unable to attend due to my involvement in a Regional Cricket event. No mention was made that day of my 23 years of service at Millfield Prep School.

I have scored and worked the scoreboard for the 1st XI for the past two summers. This I have been delighted to do. It is also a measure of the respect I have for Simon Wynn and Dave Beal and for the years of support and friendship they have always afforded me.

These two seasons – 2014 and 2015 – saw the 1st XI victorious in the Bunbury Cup, defeating Bromsgrove School (by 10 wickets) and King Edward's Birmingham (also by 10 wickets). Despite the fact that I had been the regular scorer during the season, the school did not offer to pay for my overnight accommodation before each of these finals at Oakham School, 200 miles away. On both occasions, parents of the players in the team got together (Mel and Nigel Hancock, Andy and Teresa Hall the primary instigators) and very kindly paid for my dinner, bed and breakfast accommodation.

In the 2014 final, only the Deputy Head of the Senior Management team turned up to watch and support the side.

In the 2015 final, nobody turned up.

Between September 2014 and March 2015, I regularly assisted in voluntary indoor cricket coaching at the school on Thursdays between 4pm and 8pm and on Fridays between 7am and 8am. On 11th September 2015, for the first session of the school year, I had to sign in, sign out, wear a label round my neck and be escorted off the premises at the end of the session. I never returned.

My first season as West U15 Team Manager – Oakham School, 1978
Front row, 2nd left, is future England wicketkeeper, 'Jack' Russell.

With my great friend and colleague, Ted Ashman.

Presenting the awards at a Junior Football event in Weston-super-Mare – 1978.

A distinguished group at the 3rd Bunbury Festival – County Ground, Taunton, in August 1989.

My first season in charge of Edgarley Hall (Millfield Junior School) 1st XI – 1992.
Captain, centre left, is Joey Barrington, son of the six times World Squash champion, Jonah.

Somerset U13s at the King's College Festival in 1998. Captain (middle of front row) is James Hildreth.

West Region U13 squad at King's College, Taunton, in 1999. Centre back row is the late, greatly missed, Graham Dilley, who was coach for the week. Far left is my co-manager, Phil Lawrence.

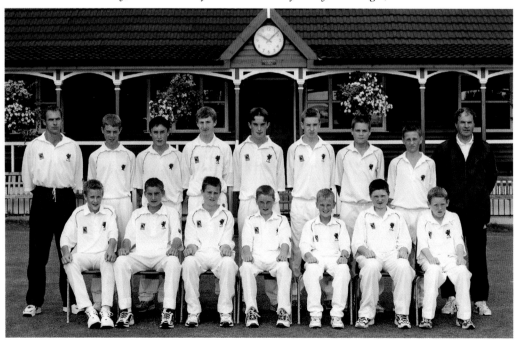

My last season managing Somerset U13s – 2000, and an unbeaten record.
I couldn't have wished for a better coach in my swansong year than Andy Hurry.

Millfield Prep School's U11 8-a-Side Hardball team, 2001. National Champions at Old Trafford.
Standing next to me is Tim Harris, co-manager/coach.

West Region U15 squad at the Bunbury Festival, Winchester, in 2001.
Far right in the back row is the coach, Paul Farbrace.

West Region U15 squad at the Bunbury Festival, Billericay, in 2002.
Far left in the back row is the coach, Keith Tomlins.

West Region U14 squad, 2005. Far left, back row, is Ian Bell.
Most of the front row have gone on to play First Class cricket, including Jos Buttler (4th from right).

With my 2006 Millfield Prep 1st XI captain, Daniel Bell-Drummond, scorer of 1,050 runs that season. Daniel is now a successful opener with Kent and is regularly mentioned in the media as a future England prospect.

Three Spanish stars of my U11B Rugby team in the Autumn Term of 2011 – Iker, Patricio, & Gervasio.

Girls U13 - National Indoor Cricket Champions, Lord's Cricket Ground, 8 May 2012.

My 2012 Millfield Prep 1st XI captain, Teddie Casterton. In a very wet summer,
he still managed to score 679 runs, including an unbeaten 104 against Colston's School.
Teddie is holding the bat awarded for his century and the Ben Hollioake Memorial Award.

CHAPTER 12

Football And Rugby at Millfield Prep

During my first term at the school, I managed the U12B Football team, Clive Thomas (Head of Athletics & Cross Country) taking the U12A side. I was impressed with the overall standard and it was satisfying to win the opening match – a 5-0 success at St Dunstan's, the local comprehensive school. Tim Harris was i/c Football and also Head of Games. During the first couple of years I assisted Tim at the C Block (now Year 6) football sessions on Thursday afternoons; I thought his technical knowledge of the game was spot-on. Tim was also a great help in coaching my U11B Rugby team during games sessions in the Autumn Terms.

Stuart Coates ran the U11 Football team when I arrived at the school before he handed over to me for the 1993 season. This has always been the age-group I've felt most comfortable with, where football is concerned, and it was the start of twenty years in charge. U11A matches (and U11B where possible) were usually played on Thursday afternoons against the local junior, primary and middle schools. In 1996 we won all ten matches played, a late winner by Josh Taplin in the final game, away to Wells Central, resulting in a trip to a local eaterie in Wells for sausage and chips. Star striker that year was James Hildreth, while in 1997 it was none other than future England Rugby captain Chris Robshaw. During the nineties, my two former junior schools in Weston-super-Mare – Milton and Worle – used to come on an annual visit to play my U11 team before partaking of 'Match Teas', the undoubted highlight of the day for most of them. At the very end of the 1997 fixture against Milton, with the score standing at 2-2, Chris scored the winner with a perfectly executed overhead bicycle kick. Even the visiting parents applauded, despite having been denied the satisfaction of a draw at 'mighty Millfield'. 1999 also saw an unbeaten season (including one or two drawn games), a keen parent producing a short video of the final match, a home win against Wells Central.

From 2000 onwards I began arranging more matches for the younger age-groups (U10, U9, U8), mostly 7 or 6-a-Side. These were usually at home and on a Wednesday afternoon, but had to be fitted in after the hockey fixtures had been completed. February 2000 saw the first of my annual U10 7-a-Side Tournaments, held on a Saturday morning, for local schools (mostly state). This was at the request of Simon Cummins and a similar event for U9 teams was started the following year. They always went down very well and, after a spell using pitches on the Spinney, were staged on ideally sized playing areas (and goalposts with nets) either side of the 1st XI Cricket square. So I always prayed for a fine day and, indeed, a dry week leading up to each tournament. I wasn't always lucky in that respect, but knew I could rely on Bob Dutton and his staff – the best in the business – to 'repair' the outfield for the start of the cricket season – which was often a mere

U9A Football, 2011-2012, MPS Tournament Winners (managed by Dave Beal)

five weeks away. A perpetual shield was awarded to the winning team along with individual medals for the winners and runners-up. Every participating player was awarded a certificate. Members of staff from the Games Department refereed the matches. Each team was given a box of ten 'goody bags', containing food and drink, for the players.

In 2006 and 2007 the school hosted the South West Region 6-a-Side U11 Tournament for state primary schools, played on those same pitches each side of the 1st XI square. It involved the twelve county winners from Cornwall up to Oxfordshire and down to the Isle of Wight. The victors here would join the three other regional winners later in the season at Wembley Stadium, playing across the hallowed turf before a Schoolboy International match. I was present for the whole day on both occasions, arranged a catering outlet to be present, unlocked doors and was on hand to ensure things ran smoothly, which I'm pleased to say they did. However, the English Schools' FA still got charged £30 an hour, which I found unbelievable. After all, this was a state schools' event and a wonderful opportunity to promote the school and to help 'fulfil its charitable status obligation'. The Headmaster told me that the ESFA could afford to pay as 'football is awash with money'. Oh dear.

During these years it was becoming more and more difficult to fit in the U11 Thursday fixtures, as the best players had to 'rest' before major hockey events (and less frequently) rugby sevens tournaments. If you fielded a weakened team against a decent junior, primary or middle school, you just got hammered. In March 2002, six of my U11A team were 'rested' three days before a hockey tournament and we lost 8-0 at Hugh Sexey Middle School, a certain Jos Buttler running the show from midfield. I wasn't happy.

Oliver Adams, son of the legendary Tony, was a striker in my 2003 team when we had a splendid record of nine wins and only a solitary defeat – to Hugh Sexey Middle School once again. Tony arrived to watch our first game, an away match against St. Paul's Junior School, Shepton Mallet, was spotted and was soon the centre of attention; a fairly orderly queue formed for his autograph (don't think selfies had been 'invented') and I'm unsure how much Tony saw of our 4-0 win, which included a goal from Oliver. All this was reported in the local paper the following week, which included a photo and Tony being described as a 'real gent'. No mention was made of the result by the way. If Tony was unable to get to a match he usually sent his driver Vic to watch and report back. In the away match against Selwood Middle School in Frome we were 5-2 down with about fifteen minutes to go. Vic called out to me that 'there's still something in this game'. Well, he was dead right as we went on to win 6-5!

In 2007, my skipper was an outstanding player from the London area by the name of Dylan Lacey. He played a major part in getting us through to the County 6-a-Side finals, but they were scheduled to be played on the first Saturday in February. This date clashed with a hockey 'block' fixture, so we had to withdraw from the football. The Lacey family later moved down from London to live in Wells. Dylan has two talented younger brothers – Finn became Head Chorister at Wells Cathedral (he is also an outstanding young actor, the lead role in 'Oliver', 'Coram Boy' and 'Les Miserables' included in

Presenting Dylan Lacey with the U11 Football Cup in 2007

his credits); while Rufus, also a talented footballer (and fellow Gooner), is a rising star at the Swindon Dance Academy.

My 2008 team lost just one of its eleven matches, playing some great 11-a-Side football. Joint captains in central midfield were Andy Tait and Conrad Lewis, who could always be relied on to put in the 'box to box' performances I always demanded of players in that position.

U11A Football, 2007-2008

I was always pleased to welcome the indefatigable Clare Blackmore to the school each year for the annual match with our U11B team with her boys (and girls) from St. Lawrence's School, followed by the highlight of the visit, sausage and chips. Clare did a great job for many years at the school, organising a variety of sporting activities for her pupils. I was also pleased to arrange, through a Millfield charity fund and the good offices of Sarah Champion, for the school to have a shed installed in the playground to store their PE and games equipment.

Angus Henderson, a proud Scot, has been Head of Football at Millfield Prep for some years now. With very little available practice time, he did incredibly well to win two National 6-a-Side titles a few years ago. However, as I said in my leaving speech, running the football department at Millfield Prep School is rather like trying to set up a Glasgow Rangers memorabilia stall outside the gates of Celtic Park, if you get my drift . . . . .

Rugby has always been my third sporting love after cricket and football but, nevertheless, I was pleased to manage/coach the U11B team for the whole of my 23 years at the school. I served under five 'A' team coaches during this time – Vaughan Williams, David Hill, Frank Maguire, Chris Kippax and Jonathan Ford. All struck me as being accomplished coaches, but each had their own individual ideas on how the game should be played. For the first couple of years, U11 rugby was 15-a-Side but then became 12-a-Side, with five forwards and the full complement of seven backs. In the early and mid-nineties the U11B didn't have that many fixtures so I used to watch the U11A team playing the likes of The Downs, Prior Park and Wolborough Hill. The standard was incredibly high, I always thought, with quick passing, strong running and 'proper' tackling around the legs. I was always willing and able to accompany the 'A' team coach to tournaments at Prior Park, Monkton Combe and Bryanston. I still keep the scoreboard going at the annual Millfield Sevens.

By 1997 the U11B team's fixture list had greatly increased to around ten matches. Half-backs that successful season were David Nuttall and Daniel Sharp, both of whom would have been 'A' team regulars at most other schools. The following year we won all eight matches, while in 1999 the team, led by Tom Wells, again did very well. In 2000, we lost the first match 14-25 to Plymouth College before going on to win the remaining nine. Ollie Hein was the star fly-half in that team with his elusive running and accurate kicking – from hand and tee. One thing which always irritated me were the occasions when opposition schools fielded quick and clever U10 players against my slower and less talented U11B lads. If you can't catch them, you can't tackle them!

In early November 1998, the U11A, U11B and 1st XV teams travelled to Bromsgrove for matches and as we pulled into the school car park, a tyre burst on a wheel of our coach. We got off, thinking that, before our return, the tyre would have been fixed. Playing on a very large pitch, my U11B team won easily by over 50 points while the U11A side, on a pitch about half the size of the one we had played on, narrowly lost. A tactical ploy by Bromsgrove which had worked. Meanwhile, on an adjoining pitch, the 1st XV had lost 7-5, their first defeat of the season. Three minutes from time they had been awarded a penalty on the 22 metre line and almost in front of the posts. Head of Rugby Bryan West (former British Lion) hated kicking of any sort and virtually banned his players from ever kicking the ball, no matter what the situation. I think if he'd had his way, he would have done away with conversion attempts after a try had been scored. However, on this occasion and seeing his unbeaten record slipping away, Bryan instructed one of his prop forwards (!) to attempt the kick at goal. The poor lad missed, of course, and the record was gone. Well, as far as I knew, nobody in the team ever practised kicking, particularly place kicks off the ground or from a tee. After match teas we returned to the coach, only to discover that it hadn't been carrying a spare wheel – apparently not legally required – and a replacement vehicle had been summoned from Somerset (Wincanton, I seem to recall) but had not arrived. It seemed we were all going to miss the school firework display at 7pm. Tears and tantrums never far from the surface. However, Bromsgrove's Head of Rugby – ecstatic at having taken mighty Millfield's unbeaten record – said the owner of the coach company in Bromsgrove who transported all their sports teams was a personal friend and, in a very short time, a luxury coach arrived to take us all back to Glastonbury and in time for the fireworks. I'm pretty sure that Millfield never received any sort of bill for the round trip of about 170 miles. By the way, in case you're wondering, the fireworks were spectacular. Incidentally, the Headmaster of Bromsgrove School at that time was Tim Taylor, who had been Head at Edgarley (as it was then) from 1978-1985, before being succeeded by George Marsh. So the school was indeed fortunate to have these two outstanding leaders at the helm for thirteen years. They were years that saw increasing numbers in the school and all round significant progress.

The number of boys in Year 6 began to decline during the early 2000s and, in recent times, it was a struggle to field two U11 sides (absolute minimum of 24 players required). Jonathan Ford has now coached the U11A team for thirteen years and, when he took over from Chris Kippax, told me there was to be no 'hiding' of probable 'A' team players in my 'B' side. Perish the thought, but point taken! Fordy was, and still is, an excellent coach, who stands behind the posts at one end of the pitch during matches, bellowing out instructions and handing out praise and constructive criticism in equal measure. With Fordy, winning very much comes second to playing the game in the right way and he certainly has no time for non-passing glory merchants. U11 rugby has now been reduced to 9-a-Side, with no set positions, uncontested scrums and no kicking at all. So posts at each end of the pitch are now superfluous, just for show. I'm sure the groundstaff will still put them up each season as Fordy would be lost without them. I mean, where would he stand during a game?

My U11B team of 2011 included three truly delightful Spanish boys – Iker, Patricio and Gervasio – who all contributed greatly to the success of that team. Iker and Gervasio were quick and elusive runners in the back division, while Patricio, as hooker – the original lovable rogue – was the best tackler I had in 23 years – and always AROUND THE LEGS. Elders and supposed betters, please note. And how their English improved between September and December. At the team photograph session in November, I got Debbi (photographer supreme) from Eric Purchase Photography to take a photo of the three boys together in their rugby kit and each was given a copy to take back to Spain. I hope each is displayed in a prominent place in their homes and that they will remember their term of rugby at Millfield Prep. Sadly, all three left at the end of the Summer Term after just a year at the school – which, I was told, had always been the plan. Being Spanish, I seem to recall that they were all talented footballers as well. . . Whatever they are now doing, I wish them well and every success in the future.

CHAPTER 13
Girls' Football And Cricket

When I was involved in primary school sport in the 70s and 80s, participation by girls in traditional boys' games such as football and cricket was discouraged. However, I do recall a girl called Catherine Herriot playing football rather than netball in games lessons at Milton Junior School, this following a parental request. Then there was Karen Stenner, who a year or two later played for the school U11B football team. I'm not sure whether this came about following a request from Karen's parents or from Karen herself – probably the latter. I got to know Karen's parents quite well and they always seemed grateful that I'd gone along with their daughter's wish to play competitive football. When Karen moved to Worle School at the age of eleven, she told me somewhat wistfully that her request to continue playing football was turned down flat. This was around 25 years ago. How times change! Incidentally, I heard from Karen in late 2013, informing me that she was now a policewoman in Bristol.

Things were much the same when I started at Millfield Prep in January 1991. Boys played traditional boys' sports and girls played traditional girls' sports. However, in 1997 there was an outstanding girl games player in Year 8 by the name of Imogen Robertson, who was probably just about good enough to be selected for that year's Cricket 1st XI – a particularly strong team that season. However, it was reckoned that for this to happen Imogen would need to 'be a boy' for the term, which would have meant her missing high profile girls' competitions in rounders, tennis and athletics. So the idea was dropped. I upset Imogen's mother that year when I called out to our fast bowler, Ben Emmett, not to carry on like an old woman during a session in the nets. Mrs Robertson marched over and told me not to make sexist comments! Something of a chastening moment. Incidentally, Imogen progressed to be an international women's hockey player.

At the beginning of the century things did begin to change. Other schools, both state and private, were starting up girls' football teams at U13, U12 and U11 and organising 6-a-Side Tournaments. Angus Henderson was pro-active in promoting and encouraging the coaching of girls' teams and preparing them for matches and tournaments. I was happy to help, as was Dave Beal. In 2005-06, an U11 6-a-Side team reached the County Finals at Yeovil. Tony Adams' daughter, Amber, was a key player for us, though we just missed out on the trophy, finishing as runners-up. The grass pitches were pretty awful and I reminded the girls how lucky they were to play on the immaculate surfaces at Millfield Prep.

The following year I was asked to take a group of Year 8 girls for football on a Tuesday after school – girls who weren't involved in National hockey or netball

U11 Girls' Football - County Runners-Up in 2006

finals later in the term. They were a determined bunch, with improving skills, who seemed to enjoy the sessions. We won a couple of tournaments and did well in the 11-a-Side matches. Katy Hancock, now a tennis coach at the school, was a super goalkeeper, while Ella McMahon (now Ella Eyre, singer/songwriter) was a feisty performer in midfield – a bit like Robbie Savage but with more skill. There was also Emily Forbat, daughter of Dr. Lance Forbat, who played a major part in saving my brother Richard's life in 2002 when he diagnosed a heart condition which everyone else seemed to have missed.

Girls' cricket was being enthusiastically (he knows no other way) coached and developed by Dave Beal; there were after-school clubs for both junior and senior girls. With rounders no longer being played as a competitive sport in the senior school, it seemed natural to phase in cricket as the main summer sport for girls. There was bound to be an overlap involving the two sports and Elaine Rawlings was determined – quite rightly – to go flat out to win the U13 National Rounders Prep Schools title, which she did for four years in a row between 2010 and 2013. Elaine also made full use of the cricket nets, both indoor and outdoor, for her many rounders practices. At the end of the 2013 season she confided to me that she would now be pleased to assist with girls' cricket at the school, only to leave Millfield Prep at the same time as myself – Christmas 2013 – to take up a senior post at a school in Abu Dhabi. Not sure if she's helping with the cricket there!

Meanwhile, Millfield Prep had begun to enter the National Lady Taverners' U13 Indoor competition and Dave Beal and I saw 2012 as the year we could go all the way and win it. Teams were 8-a-Side and we had a pretty decent squad of ten girls. Emily Bayliss – already a county player and the first winner of the Girls' Cricket Cup at school, donated by Dave and myself – was an excellent player and the ideal captain, while Georgie McTear was also outstanding. Georgia Dimdore-Miles was a very competent 'keeper, while Lauren Dolan and (the amazing) Grace Stableford were great prospects from Year 7. I had done my usual bit to persuade Emma Bedford to join the school in January and she would turn out to be another important player. Roxy Gillespie was another vital part of the team. Lucia Spencer, Emily James and Stasi Knight – all very competent performers – made up the squad. Our target was Lord's – the Home of Cricket – and the National Finals there in May.

We began by winning the District competition at the end of January, held at Hazlegrove Prep (defeating the host school in the process and who would go on to win at Lord's in both 2014 and 2015), followed by a decisive win in the County competition at Somerset's Centre of Excellence in Taunton at the beginning of March. We'd got this far with very few practices as most of the girls were heavily involved in both training sessions and tournaments in their traditional sports of hockey and netball.

The Regional finals were set for the first Wednesday of the Summer Term and were to be held at Exeter University's Cricket Centre. This Wednesday is always the beginning of the boys' outdoor season and I remember thinking that it would be a hot, sunny day and that we would be stuck inside. In the event, most of Devon had two inches of rain that day, but inside our girls were doing incredibly well. Except for the second match ending in a tie, we won all the other games and were through to Lord's. Dave Beal had done brilliantly to get us through to the finals, particularly, as I've said, with so few practice sessions. However, a much bigger problem was about to confront us and seriously endanger our chances of being National champions.

The big day at Lord's was to be Tuesday 8th May, just thirteen days after the Regional Finals. However, on Thursday 25th April I was informed that three of the girls – Emily Bayliss, Roxy Gillespie and Stasi Knight – could not play at Lord's because they had to sit INTERNAL Scholarship exams for Millfield on Tuesday 8th May and Wednesday 9th May. Could not the date of the finals be changed, someone asked? Well, that would be a bit like Arsene Wenger asking the FA if the date of the Cup Final could be changed as he had been invited to open a Garden Fete at Chalfont St. Giles on the same day. I immediately contacted the Headmistress by e-mail but she merely passed the problem onto the Senior School to be considered by Dr Fran Clough, Director of Studies and former England rugby international. On Saturday 28th April, Dan Close, Deputy Head at Millfield Prep, gave me the news that Dr Clough wouldn't budge on the matter and that the girls had to sit their Scholarship exams on the appointed days. This from a so-called sporting school.

Having had no help or backing from either school, my only hope was to get the parents onside; usually a shrewd move. Stasi's parents were keen for her to sit her exams on the appointed days (which was fair enough), but those of Emily and Roxy wanted their daughters to play at Lord's in this, as they put it, once in a lifetime opportunity. Both girls were vital members of the team; Roxy's father Stuart, an Army officer, was particularly supportive and, being a Yorkshireman, I guessed he would say that cricket should come first.

About a week before the Lord's date, I finally got the news that the girls COULD now play, BUT –

The examinations due to be taken by the two girls on Tuesday 8th May would have to be taken on Monday 7th May (May Day). I was to be the invigilator in what turned out to be the SKY television room above Dan Close's office.

From the moment the two girls went into their first exam, there was to be no contact between them and anybody else. Mobile phones and other electrical devices were taken from them. Lunch and other refreshments were brought to that upper room during the day. The usual May Day festivities were going on outside and I did well to sneak up ice creams for the two girls.

At 4pm on that Monday, Dave Beal, myself and the other seven girls left school in a minibus to travel to London and stay in a somewhat spartan and gloomy

Travelodge in Acton, West London. Dave thought he had stayed there before, but wasn't sure. At the same time, the two Scholarship girls went in a separate minibus with Chantal Collins and two female 'gappies' to stay, so I was later told, in a rather nice hotel in Swiss Cottage, an upper-crust area of North London and fairly close to Lord's. There was a rumour that the parents of the two girls had to pay for the hotel accommodation but nobody seemed sure about this and it was never confirmed one way or the other.

Ironically, both Emilys were 13 on that very day, so I ensured that a birthday cake was on hand in both the Travelodge and the hotel. It was somewhat surreal in that dingy Travelodge, singing 'Happy Birthday' and eating birthday cake around 10pm.

Tuesday 8th May turned out to be bright and sunny, but we were indoors in the Lord's Academy and determined to win the day against the other seven competing schools from all over England and Wales. Dave did his usual excellent warm-up but we didn't start well, losing to Bromsgrove by just 2 runs, and, in fact, at the lunch break had lost two of the three games played. After a guided tour round the Home of Cricket, we knew that we had to win every match in the afternoon session to secure the trophy; and that's exactly what happened. Ironically, we had to play our opening game victors, Bromsgrove, in the final. In a thrilling, epic contest, we won by just 7 runs and we were National champions. What a day – or rather two days! England Women's captain Charlotte Edwards

MPS Girls Triumph at Lord's, May 2012. Centre is Charlotte Edwards.

presented the awards and many photographs were taken of the team in their smart, much admired Woodworm kit (worn by the 1st XI boys in their National T20 success three years earlier).

It was a happy drive home and we celebrated at Fleet Services McDonald's in the traditional way. Emily and Roxy were already fully focussed on their following day exams, of course.

It was both interesting and noticeable that none of the school hierarchy came to watch; possibly they didn't think that we would win or that the event wasn't that important. After all, it was only girls' cricket.

Girls' cricket has since continued to flourish at the school under Dave Beal's infectious and enthusiastic coaching. In 2015-2016 no fewer than nine Millfield Prep girls were in the Somerset Girls' Winter Cricket Programme; three of them, in fact, are already county players.

CHAPTER 14
Touring

I completed my twenty-seventh, and possibly final, overseas Cricket Tour on 20th December 2014, although it was my first to India. Without exception, they have all been wonderful, unforgettable experiences. Seventeen of them have been entirely due to Malcolm Broad MBE, who had the foresight to set the wheels in motion and then superbly arrange and organise them all. Administrative brilliance. I can never thank him enough. It all started with four Regional tours to Holland between 1988 and 1991, prior to, can you believe, twenty-one annual tours to the West Indies between 1989 and 2010. I was fortunate to be part of thirteen of them, but more of them later.

The idea of the Dutch tours, which took place mid/late August, was to prepare and have a look at players prior to U15 Regional selection a year or two later. We took a couple of minibuses on the overnight ferry from Harwich to the Hook of Holland and stayed in a hotel in Noordwijk on the coast.

On the first trip, Bob Gabriel and I stayed in a guest house as there wasn't enough room for everyone at the hotel.

The final winner of the Bob Gabriel Memorial Award, Lewis McManus in 2010

Bob very sadly died in September 1989, just over a year after that first tour, when only in his fifties. He had been a hard-working and popular official of the Bristol Schools' Cricket set-up for a number of years and has since been sadly missed in many ways. In 1990, Malcolm Broad and I set up 'The Bob Gabriel Memorial Award', given annually to the Region's U15 'Player of the Year' – not necessarily the best performer, but a really 'good egg' and 'ideal tourist'. Somerset wicketkeeper Gary Hector was the first recipient in 1990, and the last, in 2010 (when the Caribbean Tours sadly ended), was another 'keeper, Lewis McManus, currently Hampshire's No. 1.

Back to the Holland Tours and Malcolm had established an excellent contact with Charles Verheyen, a senior figure in Dutch cricket administration. In the early years of the now legendary King's College County Cricket Festivals, the Dutch often brought over a team to compete in one of the age-groups, usually U13. My Somerset U13 side invariably 'shared' a boarding house with them, which was always very much a double-edged sword. On the one hand, the Dutch were generally so poorly (mischievously?) behaved that my Somerset lads, however hard they tried, couldn't be as bad; but, on the other hand, it meant that me and my team struggled to get very much sleep during the week.

However, I've always admired the Dutch for their approach to sport and life in general. I suspect they were always grateful to the British for the support we gave them in World War 2. One evening during a Festival, Charles Verheyen told us of his experiences as a prisoner of war at Buchenwald Concentration Camp. We talked about that long weekend in May 1940 when Germany invaded Holland on Friday the 10th; the following day Winston Churchill became British Prime Minister, while on the Sunday and Monday of that Whitsun weekend a top secret operation was carried out to rescue the large stocks of industrial diamonds from Amsterdam before the Germans got hold of them.

The four tours to Holland – two at U14 and two at U13 – were all very successful. As you might imagine, grounds were very flat, the pitches artificial and we all felt the trips were of great value and certainly served a purpose. When it was not possible for these to continue, Malcolm continued to organise – as he had done in the eighties – winter weekend coaching courses in Cornwall for West Region hopefuls from Cornwall, Devon, Dorset and Somerset. There would also be similar weekends in the north of the region, usually in the Cheltenham area, for boys from Avon, Gloucestershire, Hampshire and Wiltshire. In late August, matches were played in Cornwall (and occasionally in Dorset) – on club grounds or at Truro School – between the two halves of the region, at U14, U13 and U12 levels. I've lost count of the times I wended my way from Somerset down to Cornwall for all of these events, through those picturesque Devon and Cornish villages, to find that everything had been superbly organised by Malcolm. Nowadays, of course, the M5 runs through Devon, while all those Cornish villages have been by-passed along the A30.

In 1989, Malcolm had the innovative and inspirational idea of a West Region Tour to the West Indies. The very first, December 1989 to January 1990, was an U16 tour, consisting of boys who had played for the region in the previous summer's Bunbury Festival at Taunton School. I had decided in October that I couldn't go as it would have meant missing the first week of the following term at Milton Junior School. The inaugural tour saw six matches played against a variety of opposition in Trinidad – winning four and losing two – with important contacts

My first Caribbean Tour -
Inspecting the wicket at the Queen's Park Oval, Port of Spain, Trinidad, January 1991

being made for future visits. On their return Malcolm told me I just had to come on the 1990-91 tour, which was to be for U15s. Well, I did go and it turned out to be the first of thirteen very happy and truly memorable tours with the West Region to the wonderful islands of the Caribbean – Trinidad, Tobago, Barbados, Guyana, Grenada, Dominica – all with their idyllic climate.

However, that first tour nearly ended in a personal calamity as, having been granted the first week off before beginning my new teaching post at Millfield Prep, I was due to start on Monday 14th January. After spending the last couple of days of the tour on Trinidad's holiday island of Tobago, we arrived at the tiny airport at around 4pm on Friday 11th January to catch the short flight to Trinidad, prior to boarding a Boeing 777 at Piarco Airport for the overnight journey to Gatwick, only to discover that the flight had been cancelled! Malcolm Broad and Andy Kent kept their heads and performed wonders, while I wept hysterically on the runway – well, not quite, but I recall feeling fairly upset. Malcolm and Andy went up to the control tower and insisted something must be done; an inter-island Liat aircraft was re-routed and made an unscheduled stop at Tobago. When it finally arrived, our party of twenty boarded the de Havilland 40 seater aircraft, only to find that there were only eighteen seats unoccupied. Andy Kent sat down in the aisle, saying that he wasn't moving until the situation was resolved. The

Airport Manager was summoned; in desperation, he looked around the aircraft and ordered a man and young boy (presumably his son) to leave at once, saying they shouldn't have been on the plane. I'm sure they were just being 'picked out', but they simply got up and meekly left. When we eventually took off, the man in the seat next to me remarked that we must be important people, as not only had the aircraft made an unscheduled stop but that the crew had gone through the safety routine for the first time in this the fourth island take-off.

We raced through Piarco Airport in Trinidad, onto the aircraft and into our Club Class seats; how our considerable amount of baggage - including sixteen cricket cases – also got on board must have been something of a miracle, but I believe it all did. The flight had been delayed about an hour to await our arrival, so we had to put up with some fairly unfavourable comments and mutterings from the other passengers – perfectly understandable. We had a rather turbulent flight back to London, the pilot explaining a slight detour had to be made as the Gulf War was imminent (it actually started the following Wednesday). We arrived safely at around 9am on the Saturday, David Martin (father of tour member Tim), kindly driving me back to Somerset. So I was able to begin my Millfield Prep School teaching career 48 hours later.

The early West Indies Tours were spent mainly in Trinidad, our base being the Kes Tours Villa in Port of Spain, situated just a few hundred yards from the

Visit to a Secondary School in Port of Spain, January 1991

Trinidad is invariably not short of rain, particularly in December and January.
Here I'm scoring under a table to keep the scorebook dry!

Test ground at the Queen's Park Oval. We usually paid a short visit to Tobago – indeed, the 1991-92 Tour began there with a match against the island's U17 side, who proved a bit too strong – before ending up in Barbados where we stayed at the Rostrevor Apartments/Hotel on the very south of the island. The Rostrevor has been upgraded over the years and it was a delightful way to end the tour in the later years with my own second floor room looking out over the Caribbean Sea. Blissful.

Just about our very first contacts on arriving in Trinidad had been Raj Ramnath and his wife Cheryl. Raj was the taxi driver who transported us all over the island in his somewhat dilapidated minibus (but of which he was rightly very proud). Another key figure in those early times in Trinidad was Forbes Persad, Secretary of the Schools' Cricket Association. On the 1993-94 tour I met the legendary Brian Lara at the Queen's Park Oval. The Trinidad Government had built a palatial residence for him overlooking the Savannah, which is reckoned to be the world's biggest roundabout. After that he was dubbed the 'Prince of Port of Spain'. The locals always seemed genuinely pleased that we'd actually visited Trinidad to play matches, rather than just touring Barbados as so many UK men's and youth teams were inclined to do. Wherever we went, we were invariably made to feel very welcome and even played matches on the Test grounds in Port of Spain, Bridgetown and Georgetown, which would have been unheard of back in England.

The very first ground we played on in Trinidad was at Aranjuez, on the outskirts of Port of Spain, where Mr Ram Singh, owner of the local shop, was very much in evidence, providing refreshments, laying on lunch and even – on one memorable occasion – a loudspeaker to welcome the players onto the ground and give a running commentary. On my first visit, I was sitting under a tree doing the scoring when I realised I was being 'attacked' from above. Looking up, I saw a monkey who was cheekily throwing nuts (or something) in my direction. Very few of the smaller grounds in the Caribbean had scoreboards – even very basic ones – but it was noticeable that spectators seemed to have a good idea of the score without crowding around my scorebook. A year or two after my first visit to Aranjuez, the two young sons of the groundsman were playing at the back of the pavilion with a very old bat and which was several sizes too big for them. Malcolm asked me to do the after-match speech of thanks and when I announced that I was going to arrange for two bats for the boys to be sent out from England, spontaneous applause broke out. Martin Berrill of Hunts County Bats in Gloucester very kindly obliged. I was also pleased to sponsor a local boy there called Raymond Lyons, providing him with a bat and pads. Members of the tour party frequently gave out cricket equipment they no longer needed, but still in good condition, to local players. It was always well received and much sought after. My very last visit to the ground was on Easter Sunday in 2010; the heat was too much for us (around 38°C) and I'm sure

With Kevin Barrett (Millfield) at the British High Commissioner's residence in Port of Spain, January 1991. Kevin is currently Head of Finance Planning and Analysis at the ACE Group

this contributed to a heavy loss. The opposition was pretty good as well.

During the tours of the nineties I always roomed with Andy Kent, who I pay tribute to for putting up with my somewhat quirky ways, such as sleeping with my suitcase on the end of my bed in order to stop insects and the like creeping into it during the night – well, I think that was the reason. Andy always acted as Tour Treasurer and I can picture him now at some Caribbean airport terminal, exchanging currencies for the players (and staff); piles of Barbados dollars, Trinidad dollars, Guyana dollars and East Caribbean dollars (plus US dollars) spread out on

Meeting Richard Branson at Antigua Airport in April 1999. He was knighted at the end of that year.

some convenient flat surface. It was no good arriving in Barbados with Trinidad currency as it couldn't be exchanged there and was looked on as worthless. Andy did a superb job and always produced immaculate tour accounts a week or so after we had arrived home. I was pleased to be at Andy and Paula's wedding in January 1998 and delighted when Andy received a message from Paula, when we were on tour in Grenada the following year, that she was expecting their first child. Becky was born at the end of 1999 and a couple of years later along came Edward. Everyone was completely devastated when news came through, late in 2015, that Ed had died following an asthma attack, aged just 13. Truly awful.

Our visits to Guyana, situated on the South American mainland, were always interesting, to say the least. The officials there were even more delighted than those of Trinidad that we had gone the extra mile to visit their country as other touring teams rarely did so. We always received VIP treatment as soon as we stepped from the aircraft; had a police escort from the hotel to the grounds (and back) for all our matches and even a plain clothed officer (armed – he once showed us his gun!) for security when we went on walkabouts. I always thought that the locals treated us with some suspicion and irritation, especially when the police held up the traffic to give us an easier passage.

On one never to be forgotten Saturday, 2nd April 2005 to be precise, the day after THAT river crossing, I woke up to torrential rain in Georgetown (Guyana can be pretty wet). Back in Somerset, my good friends Janette and Steve were getting married in perfect weather. However, the rain stopped mid-morning, the sun came out and we delayed our visit to Bourda to watch the third day of the Test match between West Indies and South Africa to have a look around Georgetown Cathedral, apparently the largest all-wooden building in the world. Inside, a nun appeared, took hold of my hand and begged me to pray for the Pope who was critically ill. He sadly passed away that evening, the funeral being the following Friday. The wedding of Prince Charles and Camilla, due to take place on that very day, was postponed for 24 hours so that Charles could attend the Pope's funeral. Why a Royal Wedding was put back a day will long be a good quiz question. Excellent seats behind the bowler's arm had been reserved for us at the cricket and this was something else which irritated the locals. A couple of them explained that fewer and fewer Tests were being played in Guyana, five (and even four) match series becoming almost obsolete (except for the Ashes, of course). On entering the ground, the players were handed various paraphernalia with instructions to make as much noise as possible; a bit different from Lord's, I thought at the time.

The Caribbean Tours were fabulous, but we had started to notice a decline in West Indies cricket in general, with more people watching the Trinidad and Jamaica national football teams than attending a Test match. Nowadays, of course, some of the top West Indies players travel the world (as mercenaries – and who can blame them) playing T20 cricket, rather than representing the West Indies. However, from a West (now South & West) Region point of view, the tours were great preparation for the forthcoming Bunbury Festival four months later, and certainly helped in team bonding and generally getting to know strengths and weaknesses.

On all the major islands we visited, Malcolm always organised visits to the British High Commission, where the dress code on the invitation was invariably 'elegantly casual', speeches were made and gifts exchanged. On my last visit to Barbados in 2010 I was privileged to meet the legendary West Indian fast bowler of the sixties, Charlie Griffith, looking pretty fit at 71. I asked him what he thought of T20 cricket and he simply replied, "It's not cricket, it's an entertainment." I have to say I'm inclined to agree.

On my first Caribbean Tour, our party consisted of sixteen players and four staff, with parents 'not welcome'. This gradually changed over the years, many parents choosing to fly out to support their sons, enjoy the climate and surroundings and look on it as a once in a lifetime opportunity to witness their offspring playing in a good standard of cricket overseas. Particularly in those early years, players were encouraged to obtain sponsors and do odd jobs to help finance the tour, all

*To meet the England West Region
Under 15 Cricket Team*

*The British High Commissioner
and Mrs Duncan Taylor*

request the pleasure of the company of

Chris Twort

for Reception

on Tuesday 3 April *at* 6:30 – 8:00pm

*Ben Mar,
Pine Hill,
St Michael, Barbados*

Dress: Elegantly Casual

*R.S.V.P.
Tel: 430 7800*

this being recorded in the annual Tour brochure. Without having carried out a detailed analysis, I reckon that, overall, we won around 65% of all the matches played; a good record when one considers that we frequently played against older opposition (Carlos Brathwaite was 21 when we played against him in 2010!) and, with a tour party of 16 (and sometimes 17, which I always thought was too many) we could never put out our best XI. The players (or their parents) had paid for the tour so we tried to ensure that everyone played an equal number of matches. I sometimes get asked who the best wicketkeeper was on all my Caribbean tours and I always go for Carl Gazzard, who kept superbly on a variety of pitches (and to a variety of bowling) in 1997. Eight years later he was Somerset's 'keeper/batsman at the Oval when they won the National T20 under Graeme Smith's captaincy.

My first tour to South Africa was in the Autumn of 1995 when I accompanied David Agutter and his Mid-Somerset Schools' team. We played a variety of opposition in Cape Town and the surrounding area; it was fascinating to see the country just 18 months into Nelson Mandela's presidency.

I even accompanied an Avon Schools' side on a tour to Canada in August 1989, where opposition teams were made up almost entirely of pretty decent Asian cricketers. A memorable visit to the Niagara Falls is still the closest I've ever got to the United States. While in Toronto, it was good to meet up with my cousin

On tour with Neil Goodman (L) and James Hildreth (R), Sri Lanka, April 2000

Frances and her husband Chris, physiotherapist and surgeon respectively in the city.

I've been delighted to accompany Millfield Senior School on six of their tours since 2000, acting as team scorer, but always happy to pay my way including, of course, a single room supplement. We've been to Sri Lanka in 2000 and 2011, South Africa in 2007 and 2009, United Arab Emirates in 2012 and India in 2014. Another tour to India was also arranged for December 2008 but was called off with barely a week to go because of the Mumbai terror attacks.

Two key figures in the organisation of these tours have been Chris Gange and Richard Ellison. Chris, who played for my Somerset U13 team as a successful opening batsman in 1996 and is now a top batsman for Bridgwater in the West of England Premier League, has been an excellent tour leader and coach on these tours; while Richard, Ashes hero in David Gower's 1985 England side, has always impressed me with the total professionalism he displays in all he does. For some years now, Richard has also been a fine, sympathetic and patient bowling coach with the Somerset age-group teams; he has now been Master i/c Cricket at Millfield for over twenty years.

Mark Davis, former Somerset left-arm pace bowler and now a well-respected

On tour with (L-R) Charlie Vickery & Alex Drew and Daniel Bell-Drummond & Nick Pang

freelance coach, came on a number of these tours; as did Tony Gange, Chris's father, David Agutter and Mark (Corps) Jones. Without exception, they were great companions on tour, enjoying a high standard of schoolboy cricket and taking home memories of visits to world famous sites – including the Taj Mahal, where I was left behind!

During Millfield's tour to South Africa in December 2007, we were playing a match at Newlands Cricket Club when Richard Ellison introduced me to Juliet Cullinan whose nine year-old son, David Scott, was joining in with the Millfield players (some nearly twice as old) in their pre-match practice. I later saw David having a net session with his coach and was impressed with his ability. Having talked with Juliet at some length, we decided that Millfield Prep would be the ideal school for David. The plan was to get him over to England for Scholarship Day in January but, for whatever reason, this never happened. I'd almost forgotten about the whole business when suddenly, out of the blue, David and Juliet arrived at the school in August 2008. David was enrolled on one of Ian Thompson's excellent Football Courses and he started the new academic year in September, soon becoming my regular U11B rugby fly half; he could kick as well! His cricket developed and he was selected for the Somerset age-group teams. However, he was often unavailable for mid-winter sessions, not to mention actual county games in the summer. It was a delight when I discovered he was a member of Millfield's India Tour party in December 2014 and I look forward to seeing him in 1st XI action during the 2016 season, his final term at Millfield. He'll be 18 in July. How time goes by.

Myself and David Scott in 2009

CHAPTER 15

Somerset Schools' Cricket Association

I have been Honorary Secretary of Somerset Schools' Cricket Association since October 1972 (elected when I was incredibly young) and during those forty plus years have seen the country with nine Prime Ministers (from Ted Heath to Theresa May), but only one monarch. I have nothing but complete admiration for Her Majesty and her totally selfless dedication to public duty. Her parachute jump, at the age of 86, to open the London Olympics in 2012 will never be forgotten . . . . .

In 1972, Somerset Schools had two county age-group teams – the U15s had been in existence since the early 1950s, but the U13s not until 1970. I became involved with the U15 side as soon as I started teaching and recall a match against Cornwall on a damp and gloomy day at Torpoint when Ian Botham scored a rapid 71 not out, with Peter Roebuck virtually a spectator at the other end. Torrential rain then ended proceedings. The year before, as a 13 year-old, Ian made his debut for the U15s in a match against Wiltshire at Corsham on 21st July. He went into bat with

Two pupils meet Ian Botham at a book signing

83

the score 1-2 in the second over and, apparently, with instructions to 'play himself in'. He was out well before lunch for 80 (a six and 12 fours), having put on 135 with Phil Slocombe. Strangely enough, Ian was very rarely 'allowed' to bowl – I believe this still irks him - which is why he wasn't often given the captaincy. Interesting, of course, that he later took 383 Test wickets.

When Somerset won their first-ever trophy – the Gillette Cup – in 1979, after 104 years of trying, the winning team that day at Lord's contained six players who had previously played for the Somerset Schools' U15 side – Brian Rose, Peter Denning, Ian Botham, Peter Roebuck, Graham Burgess and Keith Jennings. Hugely satisfying to people like me. Chairman of the Somerset Cricket Board, Andy Curtis, sums the situation up perfectly in the latest Somerset Almanac when he says that 'our team frequently contains seven or eight West Country players, a far higher home grown percentage than most other counties'.

Three schoolteachers who were hugely instrumental in the development and progress of the Somerset Schools' Cricket Association in the fifties, sixties and seventies were Reg Pitman (Hon. Secretary), Frank Steer (Chairman) and Gordon Russell (Hon. Treasurer). When there was just an U15 team to select, there would be five District Trials in the county (Bath, Weston-super-Mare, Bridgwater, Taunton and Mid-Somerset), followed by North and South Trials and then a Final Trial. Reg, Frank and Gordon attended all eight trials and were known to be very thorough in their selections. Well, they selected me in 1961! In the early fifties, Bristol Schools were the solitary opponents, followed by Devon, Gloucestershire and Hampshire. Cornwall joined the list in 1959 and then Dorset and Wiltshire in 1966. The county matches (all day/declaration format, with lunch and tea intervals) were played in the first two weeks of the summer holidays, home one year, away the next. It was unheard of for parents to come and watch games (all midweek, never on a Sunday) as dads were at work and mums were at home looking after their pre-school children and doing the housework. Sorry, but I'm merely reporting the way it was. Players were transported to matches by an elaborately devised system of pick-ups and lifts in the cars of Reg, Frank, Gordon, Bob Spiller from Yeovil and myself. No Health & Safety, Risk Assessment, seat belts, etc. in those days, while players had the minimum of equipment – unlike today.

Frank Steer passed away in 1975, but I was still able to rely on Reg and Gordon (both had now retired) in improving and increasing the U15 fixture list. In 1977, 1979, 1981 and 1983 we undertook tours of the London area, playing Hampshire first, before moving on to play Middlesex, Essex and London Schools. We travelled up in Andrews Coaches of Frome and stayed in small hotels. The 1977 did not start well when it was discovered I had booked our party into a 'commercial' hotel in Romford Road, rather than its sister or family hotel half a mile away. Mark Davis, a member of the tour party, will elaborate if you ever meet him.

In the early 1980s, we started playing county matches at U11, U12 and U14 and appointed managers/coaches to look after each of the five age-group teams (myself with the U13s). The very first County U11 match was played away to Devon on Thursday 23rd June, 1983 at Tavistock Cricket Club. Our '12' for the game included the Parsons twins, Keith and Kevin, both still U10, and, interestingly, only two players from private schools. We batted first and, at tea, had scored 225-6 on an artificial wicket. I umpired at one end and former England bowler Bob Cottam at the other – one of his sons was playing for Devon. In those days, it was unheard of to have appointed umpires for junior matches, even at county level. It was not until the nineties that the situation changed and 'proper' umpires became the norm for inter-county games, knock-out finals and festivals at Taunton School and King's College. Even public schools now have their 'appointed umpire' for the season, whereas before the Master i/c usually officiated. Back to that Tavistock game and while we were all tucking into tea, the heavens opened, we had rain of Biblical proportions and virtually the entire playing area became a lake. So that was that; at least eight of our players had batted and a start had been made.

The Somerset U13 team started life in 1970 with a match against Bristol Schools at Brislington School on Saturday 11th July, which ended in a well contested draw. The following year, in the return game at Yeovil, a diminutive off-spinner by the name of Neale Oliver from Weston Grammar School recorded the remarkable figures of 10-9-1-5 and we won very comfortably by 9 wickets. However, in 1973 and 1974, we lost both matches to Bristol, their off-spinner, Gary Hall, taking 7-25 in the first game and 7-20 the following year. I've long contended that a good spinner will always trouble young batsmen, even top order ones. Somerset U11 Coach Dan Hodges used to get left-arm spinner Jack Leach to open the bowling in county games, mesmerising the opposition batsmen, totally uncertain as to how to play him. This has also been very noticeable when taking 15/16 year-olds on overseas tours. The opening pair gets to 60-0 off 10 overs against their useful but not frighteningly quick opening attack. Then the spinners come on and the next 10 overs see 18 runs scored and two or three wickets lost.

In these early years the U13 team was being picked following a two day Residential Course at Kilve Court in the West Somerset Quantocks, held over the Spring Bank Holiday weekend. However, it soon became apparent that this was unfair on those who couldn't attend and I began to organise trials and have warm-up fixtures against the likes of Millfield Foals, Taunton Cricket Club (usually at the County Ground) and, eventually, Edgarley Hall (my very first visit there was in 1980). Throughout the seventies, Avon (who had replaced Bristol), Cornwall, Devon, Gloucestershire and Hampshire were all added to the fixture list.

During this time I received much help and advice from Paul Wickham and Peter Robinson. Although Paul was an English master at Taunton School, he was

Somerset Schools' U13 squad at the NatWest Taunton School Festival in 1990.
Front row, 2nd right, is Luke Sutton, later to have a successful career as a wicketkeeper / batsman
with both Derbyshire and Lancashire.

Hon. Secretary of the Somerset Cricket Association with special responsibility for the junior sections of clubs – which were beginning to thrive out of necessity with the demise of cricket in many state schools; and not forgetting the grammar schools being turned into comprehensives and the cricket squares into staff car parks, or whatever. Paul would frequently send me long, always helpful, letters in his distinctive handwriting, often advising me to take a look at this player or that player who attended non-cricket playing schools. Paul was an ideal choice as Organising Secretary of the third Bunbury Festival, based at Taunton School, carrying out his role with his customary efficiency. Sadly, Paul is no longer with us, having succumbed to Motor Neurone Disease a few years ago. Mike Ward, Master i/c Cricket at Taunton Junior (now Prep) School for many years, organised a superb Festival Dinner on the Thursday evening. Mike also managed various Somerset Schools age-group teams, always preferring, naturally enough, the U11s.

Former Somerset player and coach Peter Robinson was another who gave me great help, not least in persuading Somerset's Head Groundsman to allow us to play the occasional county match or use as a venue for an age-group county final. Alan Ranger and Colin Jones were also indebted to Peter for enabling the Ewart Hebditch Finals to also take place on the County Ground. Peter, knowing that for a number of years I was very much a one man band running the County U13 Schools' side, would frequently turn up to lend support and offer much-valued advice. Apparently, Peter and Ken Palmer meet up every Saturday morning throughout the year at Peter's allotment for a coffee and chat – putting the world to rights and, not least, Somerset cricket. I first met up with Ken when son Gary was going through the age-groups with Somerset Schools. After leading the West to success in the 1981 U15 Festival (pre-Bunbury), he went on to captain the England U15 side later that summer. After being such an outstanding schoolboy cricketer, it's hard to understand why Gary never quite made it as an established county player. However, he has become a very successful and innovative coach, running his own Cricket Academy in Oxfordshire. Ken, former Somerset all-rounder and Test umpire, has been a much valued colleague in recent years, always keenly interested in youth and schoolboy cricket and willing to offer the benefit of his wide knowledge and experience. Ken and I are now often to be found watching Somerset cricket from the Long Room at the County Ground

Between 1990 and 1993, my U13 team enjoyed competing in County Festivals at Taunton School – initiated and organised by Paul Wickham – before the festivals were moved across Taunton to King's College, where they have remained to this day. Throughout the late eighties and early nineties, I reckoned to play around 14 county matches a season, which include a three or five match festival at King's. In the matches leading up to the festival, I used to play 5 ½ hour matches, starting at 12 noon, packed lunch at 1.30, followed by two 2 hour sessions from 2.10. Tea was provided at 4.10. Proper ('declaration') cricket.

In 1991, we played Devon U13s at the old Tone Vale Hospital – now a housing estate – and came up against an outstanding 12 year-old wicketkeeper/batsman in Chris Read. Two years later Chris was in the West U15 side, having toured the West Indies earlier in the year, but it was David Nash who was selected for the National team. Chris should have played many more times for England and I've always considered that he was very poorly treated by Duncan Fletcher.

During my time as Somerset Schools' Secretary I have always organised the various age-group knock-out Cup Competitions. It started off with just the U15s, but by the time we reached the year 2015 the number had risen to seven. I need to get the U15 (T20) competition done and dusted by mid-June so that the winning school can go through to the regional stages in late June/early July; the U14 and U12 competitions need to produce a winner by the end of term (or September!) to qualify for National U15 and U13 events the following year. At U13 it's the Frank Steer Memorial Shield, which needs to be settled by the end of term. Then there's the U11 8-a-Side Hardball competition, when I need a county winner to go through to the regional stage on the third Monday in June; this competition also has a Plate section for state schools; finally, there's the long-established Ewart

Hebditch Cup, pairs cricket for state junior, primary and middle schools (U11), using a softball. Besides the team trophy for the winning team at each age-group, there are medals for all the players, winners and runners-up, in the various finals.

CHAPTER 16
Somerset Cricket Board

In 1996, the Somerset Cricket Board was set up and took over all responsibility for youth and recreational cricket in the county. This meant the end of the Somerset Cricket Association but, after being in existence for exactly fifty years, I was both anxious and determined to keep the Somerset Schools' Association going – which I'm pleased to have done for the past twenty years. I'm very grateful to Andy Curtis (Chairman) and John Davey (Treasurer) for all the help they have given me in achieving that aim. Between 2007 and 2013 I compiled all the Cricket Board's age-group fixtures.

I was happy to continue managing the U13 side under the Board's umbrella, but was now assigned a team coach; the two-legged variety rather than the motorised one. We also resurrected the Home Counties Tour over the Spring Bank Holiday weekend, consisting of four matches against strong county opposition. Paul Wickham had first started similar tours with the Somerset Cricket Association U13s twenty years earlier; in 1986, with the Parsons twins, Keith and Kevin in their line-up, they defeated Essex by 10 wickets (after bowling them out for 70), a result which, I understand, sent shock waves through that county. Here I must give a mention to Haydn Davies, who has been compiling the Essex age-group fixtures since 1961 – all done by telephone and letter. Dates, grounds, catering, umpires all in place in good time; barely a hiccup, I should imagine, in all those years. When he finally retires, we will never see his like again. By the way, Haydn is also the Essex Schools General Secretary and organises all the competitions.

I managed the Somerset Cricket Board U13 team for five years, achieving some excellent results with some very good players. As previously mentioned, Chris Gange was a highly successful opening bat in 1996 and a fine innings of 78 from him at Brentwood helped us defeat Essex by 8 wickets. The following year I will always remember an innings of 92 by Joe Becher in an away match against Warwickshire on a hard, fast, bouncy wicket. Joe was slight in stature and the opposition quick bowlers really fancied their chances against him, but his innings, which lasted 201 minutes, proved to be a match winning one. Other scores that season included 67* v London Schools, 65 v Essex, 94 v Berkshire, 63 v Gloucestershire and 70 v Worcestershire. Two years earlier I had seen Joe and Philip Read put on an unbroken first wicket stand of 225 for Somerset U11s against a good Cornwall team at Werrington (both boys scoring centuries and using M&H bats, which were coming into fashion). Back to the U13 side in 1997 and I was lucky to have an outstanding opening attack in Gareth Andrew (later to have a decent career with Worcestershire) and Nick Gerrish from Wells. Devon had us all out for 80 on the first Saturday in July before Gareth and Nick skittled them for just 21.

James Hildreth, along with three Bridgwater boys – Steve Davis, Andy Hallaran and Daryl Cocks – were mainstays of another very good side in 1998. I also had an excellent opening bowler in Michael Parsons. When we played Worcestershire at Millfield Prep in July, the opposition arrived with a record of never having lost a county game since being formed as U11s two years earlier. We bowled them out for 127 in 50.2 overs (!), Hildreth taking 4-16 and Wellington off-spinner Paul Short 3-23. With plenty of time to get the runs, James Hildreth was anxious, nevertheless, to get the match won quickly; his unbeaten 108 (out of 130-1) with 18 fours and a six, duly did so. Great credit to Steve Davis at the other end who very unselfishly gave as much of the strike as he could to James to enable him to reach his ton.

Before the first match of the 1999 season I informed the players that their playing record as members of the U11 and U12 Somerset squads had been pretty awful. Some of them looked a bit shocked at my bluntness, but it must have had some sort of an effect as we lost only one game all season – and that in the final over against Lancashire when our last man was given out LBW (apparently an inside edge onto pad). Essex, Gloucestershire, London Schools, Wales and Worcestershire were all defeated.

The 2000 team was a truly outstanding one, being undefeated in the fourteen matches played, winning the six-county festival at King's College and being runners-up in the West Counties U13 Championship. The squad included four boys who would go on to play First Class cricket – Robin Lett, Rob Woodman, Sam Spurway and Max Waller – while Liam Lewis became a regular opener for Devon in the Minor Counties. 'Gus' Fraser-Harris was an excellent captain and, to top it all, the legendary Andy Hurry was the team coach. In cricketing terms, Andy and I were 'made for each other' where running a young cricket team was concerned and I'm so pleased that he went on to become Somerset's Head Coach before becoming Head of the England Development Programme, a job which includes looking after the England U19 side.

At the end of August that year, I entered a Somerset U13 'B' team in a King's College Festival - two Welsh counties and Berkshire were also there. This age group had strength in depth that year and after we had won I decided it was probably the right time to 'retire' and hand over the manager's job to somebody else. Since the founding of the U13s in 1970, I had missed only a handful of all their fixtures, whether Schools (mostly) or Cricket Board. It had taken a lot of my time but I had no regrets at all. It had been a pleasure and a privilege to be involved with so many outstanding young players at that level.

Receiving my Honorary Life Membership from Michael Hill (L) and Peter Anderson (Middle)
December 2000

In December of 2000 I was made an Honorary Life Member of Somerset County Cricket Club for 'services to schools and youth cricket'. I was so proud and if there was one thing that I could somehow relay to my late father then this would be it. I'm sure he would be equally proud. There are only about thirty of us, around half being distinguished former players and the other half those like me who 'had done the slog' – but with a huge amount of enjoyment and pleasure along the way. I understand that the late and greatly missed Tony Davies was the prime mover behind my Life Membership, supported by Chief Executive Peter Anderson.

Between 2001 and 2003, parents of players who represented the county U11 side often told me that when they went to watch their son playing in matches against other south-west counties they discovered that the opposition players were more experienced and 'streetwise', simply because they had played a season of U10 county games the year before. Why didn't Somerset have an U10 team?

In the autumn of 2003 I arranged one or two provisional U10 fixtures for the following summer and put forward my plans at a Youth Committee meeting in January. Opinions were somewhat divided but Tony Davies, SCB Chairman at the time, possibly sensing I was looking a bit upset at some of the negativity, said to me to go ahead with a small number of fixtures and a review would take place at the end of the season. Andy Curtis was also in favour, as was Peter Anderson, who sent me a positive note. However, Performance Director Pete Sanderson was against the idea and sent me a list of conditions which would have to be met if this U10 plan of mine was to go ahead. Well, I decided that I couldn't go along with this, so between 2004 and 2012 the County U10s was a 'rebel' team (as Alun

Jenkins named it), made up of boys from private and prep schools in Somerset and following a trial – including the Bath and North Somerset areas. However, if a reliable source nominated a boy from a state school he would have a good chance of being selected. Two examples of this happening are George Bartlett and Todd Barrett; another is Ben Mason, who was an outstanding wicketkeeper in the 2007 team.

The 'rebel' team played around six games a season against neighbouring county U10 sides, home matches usually played at Millfield Prep. I was very much a one man band, although did get some help with pre-match coaching from Dave Beal and his elder son Josh. Dave's younger son Sam played in the team for three years. The 'rebels' got no publicity – reporting of matches and so on – in the local press or in the Somerset Year Book as I was conscious we weren't a recognised team. No match fees were charged so players were getting free cricket of a decent standard; they even received a team shirt at no cost. Between 2010 and 2012 these shirts were kindly supplied by Somerset County Sports and we were on our way to being recognised by the County Board. We were also getting a coach for most games, thanks to the good offices of Alun Jenkins and Jimmy Cook. After some discussion, the 'rebels' were no more, we were integrated into the system and Somerset U10s were officially the county's youngest age-group team. It was with a feeling of some pride when we attended, for the first time, the Cap Presentation evening at the County Ground in early May. We had arrived and been accepted. Strangely enough, in a way, I've always said that the best 'rebel' team I ever had was the last one in 2012 when we had a talented and balanced team of quick bowlers, spinners and batsmen. Unfortunately, that season was a very wet one and virtually every match was rain affected.

So from 2012-13 the U10 team was selected from a squad which had undertaken seven indoor winter sessions; this after District trials at four centres followed by a final trial on the Friday; all this having taken place in the late October half-term week. In 2015, the U10 team won seven matches out of ten, which was highly commendable as development comes before results. Right from the beginning in 2004, U10 county games have invariably been 35 overs a side, giving batsmen the chance to build an innings without feeling the need to slog. A good example of this was seen at Worcester in 2015 when Noah Davis and Ollie Hunt came together at 16-3 and patiently put together a stand of 126. Although we've had one or two disagreements, mainly over selection, Greg Kennis continues to do an excellent job as Head Coach. "You're not a one man band any more, Tworty, so we may have to rein you in a bit!" Point taken.

After three years managing the official U10s, I have now been 'promoted' to the U11s for 2016. So Will Crane, Ollie Heard and Josh Thomas will have had to put up with me as their manager for three years in a row. Sorry about that, lads!

CHAPTER 17
English Schools' Cricket

As Hon. Secretary of Somerset Schools I attended the annual meeting of the representatives of the south-west counties, usually held on a Sunday in September and in one of the Taunton public schools. It was invariably a useful meeting and ended up with a fixture making session. In 1977 I was invited to help manage the West U15 team in the National Festival, based at Shiplake College in Berkshire. The team manager was Peter Lewin of Hampshire and I was given the impression that they wanted me to take over from him the following year. Up until now, Somerset had rarely put forward nominations for this side, apparently saying that it clashed with their county programme. This year, however there were four Somerset boys in the squad of 13, one of whom, Michael Roe (wicketkeeper/batsman) by name, joined the police force, rose quickly through the ranks and eventually became a Commander (I think) in Bristol.

My first year as West Region U15 Team Manager - Oakham School, 1978.
Standing next to me is my captain, Adrian Dunning of Millfield School.

The following year, Peter Lewin was ousted – somewhat unfairly, I thought, but the West's England selector, Brislington School Headmaster John Hellier, seemed determined to get him out – and I was installed in his place. The 1978 Festival was held at Oakham School and, except for future England wicketkeeper Jack Russell, we had a pretty weak side. In fact, only sixteen boys turned up for the solitary trial at Exeter School, three of them being 'keepers. In those days, the eight West counties (we rarely heard from Dorset and Wiltshire) were invited to nominate boys for a trial which took place just a week before the festival. I'm not sure what we would have done if it had rained on the trial day. We lost the first two games at Oakham, but did at least earn an honourable draw against the North in the final match.

We were much stronger in 1979 when the festival was held in Durham and when most of our party travelled up by train. Included in our squad were future England rugby player and coach Andy Robinson, future England fast bowler David 'Syd' Lawrence (who arrived in damp Durham without studded footwear, but we managed to sort that), Paul Roebuck (younger brother of Peter) and Nick Folland from Devon, who was to be captain. We beat the Midlands in the first game, lost to the South in the second, while the North match was rain ruined. After a delayed start, we lost the toss, were put into bat and, against their usual battery of quick bowlers, Nick Folland scored a very fine half century. It certainly clinched his place in the England U15 side that year. Soon after the North had started their innings it rained again and the match was abandoned. Nick went on to score thousands of runs for Devon in the Minor Counties, had three seasons with Somerset and is now Headmaster of Sherborne Prep School in Dorset.

The 1980 Festival took place at the Boots ground in Nottingham, just up the road from Trent Bridge. Ours was a fairly average side and we were well beaten

With ESCA colleagues at a representative match at the County Ground in Taunton.
L to R: Leslie Fellows, John Weitzel, Roger Truelove, self, Richard Harding.

in the first two matches against the Midlands and North. The evening before the third game I made an impassioned speech to the players, telling them that if we lost to the South I was liable to be sacked – rather like a football manager whose team has just lost seven in a row and is hovering above the relegation zone. Well, we did win, or rather 14 year-old Gary Palmer won it, almost on his own. He top scored with 62, then took 6 wickets, a catch and ran somebody out. Job intact.

Gary was captain the following year in the festival held in Lincolnshire. We drew a high scoring game on the first day (when Charles married Diana – I know, I need to get out more), before a decisive win against the North on Day 2, when our spinners (Alan Buzza and Nick Walters) bowled them out. We drew with the South on the final day, but a win and two draws were enough to give us the title – for the first time since the Bristol Festival in 1973.

We thought we had a decent team for the 1982 Festival, held at St. Helens on Merseyside, but our two major run scorers (or so we were hoping), Nick Pringle of Somerset and Hampshire's Jon Ayling, didn't perform as expected and results were disappointing. The following week, Pringle scored two county hundreds and Ayling 180+ against Somerset U15s at Wells. Both players went on to have brief First Class careers, Ayling's cut short by injury.

In October of that year, John Stevens, who had taken over from John Hellier as England selector for the West, was elected as Vice-Chairman of ESCA, meaning there were vacancies for the West representative on ESCA's National Executive and for England selector for the West. In an election for these two positions among the eight West counties, Malcolm Broad was elected onto the ESCA Executive, while I got the England job.

As mentioned in Chapter 14, Malcolm had been very busy doing valuable groundwork at U12, U13 and U14 levels, in the form of coaching weekends and internal festivals, to better prepare West teams for the U15 Festival. We also had to improve our selection methods and adopt a more professional approach, suspecting that, in the past, good players had somehow been missed. Malcolm, John Stevens and I also thought that the other three regions looked on us almost as makeweights (except in 1981) and their best chance of a win. Well, we were determined all that was going to change.

In the very first over of the 1983 Festival, based at Caterham School in Surrey, we dismissed the North's Michael Atherton for 0. However, they made something of a recovery and we ended eleven runs short of their total for the match to end as a draw. We lost a low scoring match against the South, for whom 13 year-old Mark Ramprakash scored 56, before a final day draw against the Midlands. So the new era hadn't begun that well, but a glance at the team lists of the four regions that year revealed names of players who would go on to become county regulars, including four who would play for England. So the standard was particularly high that year.

In 1984, all Malcolm's preparation really paid off when we won two and drew one match in the Hull Festival, superbly organised by Ken Lake, and were crowned champions. It was very fitting, I thought, in John Stevens' year as ESCA Chairman. Our talented and extrovert captain, Somerset and Millfield's Harvey Trump, sent over champagne to our table at dinner. Now that's what I call style.

The 1985 and 1986 Festivals, held in Cornwall and at Rugby School respectively, were almost ruined by heavy rain. In 1987, Bunbury arrived in the shape of David English – but more, much more, of that in the next chapter.

Helicopter attempting to dry the pitch at the ESCA U15 Festival at Helston CC, Cornwall - 30th July 1985

Back to 1983 and the first of fourteen happy and rewarding years as an England U15 selector. Derek Day of Lancashire and the North was the Team Manager and my fellow selectors that year were Mick Verney (Surrey and the South) and Mike Hodgkins (Nottinghamshire and Midlands). Jim Bowden (Essex) soon took over from Mick Verney, while Mike Rowson of Norfolk had spells taking over from Mike Hodgkins.

With a reputation for being a somewhat dour Lancastrian, Derek Day tended to look on me with an air of suspicion initially, but as soon as he realised I wasn't a complete idiot and knew something about the game, we got on really well. When the final two days of the festival saw England U15A play the President's XI and England U15B play England U14 (managed for a few years by Malcolm Broad),

Derek always insisted I went with him for the 'A' game, leaving the other two selectors to do the 'B' match.

The match programme was the same for many years. Following the two day contest against the President's (Hubert Doggart's) team, two day matches followed against Wales U15 and Scotland U16, away one year, home the next. We always went up to Scotland in the odd years and across the bridge to Wales in the even ones.

The two star names in the 1983 England U15 team were Michael Atherton and Nasser Hussain. Both were outstanding batsmen and, can you believe, leg-spin bowlers. However, although Atherton bowled regularly throughout his school and university career (at Cambridge) his back problem was getting worse and worse and he became a batsman only. Nasser started in the Essex age-group teams at the age of eight as a leg-spinner and useful bat. He took a lot of wickets at all levels until, when in his teens, he had a massive growth spurt, 'lost the art of flight' and wasn't bowling regularly enough to progress. Derek Day surprised everyone that year by picking Hussain and not Atherton as captain; I understand that Athers still moans about this 'injustice' in the Sky commentary box. At the end of the first day of the Scotland match, played at Hamilton Crescent in Glasgow, we had the home team following-on. However, on the second day their No.7 scored a century and the match was drawn.

In 1984, Somerset and the West's Harvey Trump was captain; the game against Wales at Briton Ferry Steel was heading for a draw on the second afternoon when

Harvey Trump and Jonathon Atkinson

Harvey took a truly memorable catch at extra cover. Derek Day almost bit through his pipe, Wales were bowled out and we won by 9 wickets.

At the end of the wet Cornwall Festival, which finished in Truro on the Friday, we had to be in Glasgow 48 hours later as the Scotland match was scheduled for the Monday and Tuesday. In a very wet summer, we did well to get in two full days of cricket at Pollok, the mystery spin of Warwickshire's David Barr proving too much for the Scots. Wicketkeeper that year was Paul Nixon. The Wales game was also drawn, despite 125 from Mark Ramprakash.

The third day of the 1986 Festival at Rugby School was completely washed out, so we had a lengthy selection meeting that morning to pick the England team. Piran Holloway of Millfield, Cornwall and the West had scored very few runs on the first two days, but I reckoned him to be a top batsman and fought very hard (and ultimately successfully) for his selection. As we came out of the meeting, ESCA General Secretary Cyril Cooper said to me, "Well, I didn't think you were going to get him in." Piran fully justified his selection by being the top run scorer in the international matches and being given the Cricket Society's Jack Hobbs Award that year. Spinners Jeremy Batty and Andrew Roberts took most wickets and were greatly assisted by the best 'keeper in my fourteen years as a National selector in Wayne Noon (11 stumpings).

The first Bunbury Festival took place in 1987 at Harrow in Middlesex and it was just as wet as in 1986 and 1985. England defeated both Wales and Scotland, the team including future Test and county players in John Crawley (who kept wicket), Aftab Habib (who spent two years at Millfield Prep), Ronnie Irani, Ben Smith and Russell Warren. It was an interesting exercise getting twelve players' 'coffins' – in fashion at the time – on the train at New Street, Birmingham, for the journey to Scotland.

After the 1988 Bunbury Festival, there was an innovation with a Northern Counties Festival on Humberside. In their three 2-day matches, England defeated Holland and drew with Wales and Denmark. Outstanding batting came from Richard Kettleborough and Jeremy Snape. Derek Day was not impressed with the standard of England's fielding and, furthermore, stated that 'many of the players were not as physically fit as they might have been'. Off the field highlight was the Festival Dinner in the Hull Guildhall. Festival Organiser Lord Humberside (aka Ken Lake) did a super job.

As the 1989 Festival in Somerset (based at Taunton School) was a week later than usual – purely for my benefit, as I was still teaching in the state system - the England U15 match with Wales was played beforehand at Shrewsbury Cricket Club, England winning by an innings. Skipper Matthew Walker of Kent scored a century, as he did in the Festival's 2-day match at the County Ground, Taunton.

*The Somerset Schools' committee who organised and ran
the third Bunbury Festival at Taunton School in 1989.
Back row (L to R): Alan Ranger, Colin Jones, Tony Amor, Roger Craddock, Mike Ward.
Front row (L to R): Peter Knott, self, Paul Wickham*

We had the longest ever trip to play Scotland, staying at Dundee, before travelling even further north to play the match at Strathmore Cricket Club, Forfar. The match was drawn and we were probably saved from defeat by a gritty 68* from James Hindson of Nottinghamshire, who had earlier taken 6-38 with his left-arm spin. Glen Chapple, who went on to have a highly distinguished career with Lancashire, spearheaded the bowling attack. I travelled back to Somerset with Cornwall's Jonathan Kent on a direct (!) train from Dundee to Weston-super-Mare.

I arrived late for the 1990 Festival at Oundle School (last year in the state system), so Andrew Kennedy kindly did my selectorial duties. Skipper for the U15s that year was Robin Weston (son of former England rugby player, Mike) and he scored 443 runs in six innings, including two centuries. We drew with Wales at Neath, before defeating the Scots at Sefton Cricket Club in Liverpool. A certain Michael Vaughan was 12th Man and took no part in either game. To his credit, I've never heard him have a moan about this, either verbally or in the press.

Worcester in 1991 saw us select 14 year-old Phil Neville instead of Marcus Trescothick (who had scored very few runs in the Festival matches). Neville and skipper Lee Marland were an outstanding opening pair in the international matches, which included a trip to Stenhousemuir to play Scotland and a series of 1-day and 3-day matches against the touring Barbados U16 team. Paul Collingwood and Vikram Solanki were members of the squad. Gordon Lord had taken over from David (Bumble) Lloyd as National U15 Coach.

After the 1992 Festival at Charterhouse School, we set off for Abergavenny for the annual match against Wales. The press and media were out in force before the start as a certain Liam Botham was in the England side. A well contested match saw Wales set England 224 to win on the second afternoon. After lunch, I took David Roberts of Cornwall along the Heads of the Valley road to Merthyr Tydfil for physio treatment, but when we returned to the match England were in trouble at 162-7. David, who normally batted at No.3, went in to join Liam Botham at the fall of the eighth wicket to try and secure a draw. However, Liam had other ideas, scored 73 not out off 61 balls with five sixes, the final one – to win the game – being struck into the garden of a nearby house off the first ball of the final over. Earlier in the match he had taken eight wickets and a somewhat distraught Wales coach was heard to mutter afterwards, "It would have to have been him." By the way, in contrast to the start of the match, the press and media were nowhere to be seen. I had proposed Luke Sutton as captain at the selection meeting and he certainly vindicated my faith in him, being outstanding both on and off the field. I've never been very keen on wicketkeeper captains unless, of course, you happen to be called Luke Sutton or Alec Stewart.

The South African U15 National team toured in August that year, playing three 3-day matches and a similar number of 1-day games. We lost the 1-day series but won the 'Tests', the victory at Derby being the only definite result.

The England side of 1993 contained five players who would go on to be regulars in the First Class game – Gareth Batty, David Nash, David Sales, Owais Shah and Alex Tudor. Due to injury, Andrew Flintoff did not feature, but was a vital member of the side which enjoyed a highly successful tour to South Africa earlier in the year – one tour I didn't go on! After a high scoring draw against Wales (David Sales 144*), we made a return visit to Hamilton Crescent. Very heavy rain meant little cricket was played, the only drama being when nine of the twelve man squad got stuck in the lift at our Glasgow University Hall of Residence. We called for help, which was a long time arriving – nearly an hour – and suspected that some of the players had started to mildly panic when we finally got them out.

Paul Franks (Notts.) led the U15 team in 1994, which was blessed with four excellent spinners, one of whom was Graeme Swann and another James Troughton (grandson of Patrick of 'Doctor Who' fame), who bowled left-arm spin, but not much for Warwickshire in later years. Stephen Peters scored 125* in a rain ruined draw in Cardiff while Scotland were beaten by 49 runs in a low scoring encounter.

After the drawn match against the President's XI at the end of a splendid Bunbury Festival in Bournemouth in 1995, we headed first to Chester to play Wales – who collapsed to 112 all out in their second innings to give us a comfortable win. My final trip to Scotland as a National selector saw a second visit to Edinburgh, where we stayed at Fettes College. Richard Dawson (now Head Coach at Gloucestershire) was an excellent captain on and off the field, while Michael Gough (now a First Class umpire) batted particularly well. As in 1993, I travelled home on the overnight sleeper, arriving in Bristol at around 6am.

My swansong came at the Oxford Festival in 1996, at the end of which we had to select a squad to represent England U15s in the first Lombard World Challenge. It was a very long meeting and I wasn't particularly happy with the final outcome. The West U14 side had been outstanding in 1995 and thought they should have had a greater representation. James Adams and John Francis (both Hampshire) picked themselves, but the likes of Wes Durston and Peter Trego missed out. There was much discussion as to whether Alex Loudon should be captain, as some thought that selecting an Eton boy might 'send out the wrong message'. The final of the World Challenge took place at Lord's, India defeating Pakistan and the match ending in a near riot when thousands of supporters from both sides raced onto the hallowed turf.

I decided it was time to go (fourteen years is a good stint), assured Derek Day it wasn't because of the result of that final selection meeting and said I would only stand down if Andy Kent agreed to take my place. I'm glad to report that he did. So ended an unforgettable era as a National selector for the England U15 team.

For around ten years there was a West Region U13 team (which included players from Wales). After a trial or two, a squad was selected to play in a festival against the other three regions at King's College in Taunton (again organised by Malcolm Broad), this usually taking place during the second week in August. Phil Lawrence and myself were joint Team Managers and Rhonda Robins was our immaculate scorer. Rhonda retired from teaching at nearby Trinity Primary School in Taunton at the end of the school year in 2015 and her enthusiasm and dedication in promoting and organising cricket in her school will be greatly missed. We had various coaches assigned to the team over the years, including the late Graham Dilley in 1999 and, more recently, Keith Tomlins. Jos Buttler was in the squad in both 2003 and 2004, while in 2005 current Bath and England rugby player Henry Thomas was an explosive opening batsman. That year we also broke new ground by having a girl in the squad, opening bowler Anya Shrubsole from Bath, and look how well she's now doing in the England Women's team.

This all ended in 2010 with re-organisation by the ECB, as did the U14 Regional

Festival at Loughborough. This had started twenty years earlier, in 1990, in Warwickshire, before moving to Oundle School and thence to Loughborough – where it usually took place the week after the U13 Taunton event. Regions found it useful for selection purposes to have a look at the talent available to them before the major event the following year in the shape of the Bunbury Festival. In 2001, the successful U15 West squad had hardly changed since the U13 Festival squad in Taunton two years earlier. In fact, the only newcomer at U15 was Graham Williams from Gloucestershire who, apparently, had hardly started playing cricket until he was 13.

The late and greatly missed Hugh Cherry organised the U14 Regional Festival for many years, doing a thankless task, often under trying circumstances. Here I'm talking about the weather. From 1999 to 2010 it was almost unbelievable the amount of rain that fell at both Taunton and Loughborough during those two middle weeks of August. So we often arrived at the two venues on a Sunday, only to see the weather forecast and a succession of Atlantic fronts waiting to pile in. At Loughborough, the cap presentation always took place on the Monday morning and, although I wasn't present every year, can never remember it being done anywhere but inside and out of the rain.

Peter Bolland ('Bolly') has been an excellent Regional coach for a number of years now and has been a great comrade and companion on the West Indies Tours. A few years ago, Paul Farbrace ('Farby') was the U15 Regional coach; I'm so delighted he is now in the England set-up, doing so well and very highly thought of. A few years ago, the late Tom Cartwright was a highly respected coach when Wales was 'joined' to the West in 1999. I remember Tom tipping a 12 year-old James Vince as one to look out for. How right he was. Currently, Steve Williams, Greg Kennis, John Derrick and Matt Drakeley are conscientious and much valued ECB coaches in the South & West organisation.

CHAPTER 18
The Bunburys

I first met David English in March 1984 when he was guest speaker at the Annual Dinner of the Londonaires Cricket Club (who sadly no longer exist) in Weston-super-Mare (birthplace of Peter Trego, John Cleese but, I have to say, few other people of note). At the end of this auspicious first meeting, my brother Richard and I showed David the nightspots of Weston before he retired for the night at the Grand Atlantic Hotel on the seafront.

Three years later we met up again when Dave and the Bunburys started to sponsor the annual U15 Festival, involving the four regions of England and Wales. Up until 1986 the Festival was in grave danger of dying on its feet and simply fading away. Although some sponsorship had come from the likes of United Friendly Assurance, County Schools' Associations who were hosting the festival

The Great and the Good. Bunbury Festival - 2012.
Jonny Bairstow is sitting on Dr Dave's right.

had to do some fundraising themselves to meet ever-rising costs. At the very first festival I attended – Berkshire in 1977 – I clearly remember players having to pay something like £15 each for the honour of representing their Region and to help towards their board and lodging cost for a minimum of four nights.

Everything changed in 1986 when the then General Secretary of ESCA, Cyril Cooper, was introduced to David by the editor of the Cricketer Magazine, Ben Brocklehurst (a former captain of Somerset). It is no exaggeration to say that, but for this meeting, the annual U15 Festival would most probably have died out some years ago.

So it all started at Harrow in Middlesex in 1987 and, since then, has simply grown and grown and got better and better. July 2016 will see the 30th Bunbury Festival, this one being held at Radley College in Oxfordshire. I understand David has locations booked up to and including 2021 (Eton College).

He has just produced a magnificent leather-bound 'bible' (540 pages) entitled 'The Bunbury ESCA Festival' – 'Celebrating 30 Glorious Years 1987-2016'. Definitely worth a read. I'm sure the great man won't mind me reproducing the book's very first paragraph –

'This book is dedicated to those very special people who have helped me create the Bunbury Cricket Club over the past thirty years. It is a book filled with love . . . love for the game, the schoolmasters, the headteachers, the coaches, ESCA, the ECB, the MCC, the sponsors, the radio, TV, press, the mums and dads . . . but, above all, the young players who have dazzled us with their talents for thirty years'.

Says it all, I'm sure you'll agree.

Since the start of it all in 1987, 1680 boys have played in the Bunbury ESCA Festival; 684 have gone on to play First Class cricket; 70 have played for England.

In 1992 the Bunburys brought over the South African U15 side to play the first 'Test' series between our two countries after South Africa's re-admission.

1996 saw the staging of the first ever U15 Junior World Cup, the Lombard World Challenge.

2000 saw the staging of the second Junior World Cup, the Costcutter World Challenge.

At U12/U13, there is the David English/Bunbury Cup Competition, whereby the 40 counties produce a winning school at U12 level, who then compete nationally the following year at U13.

Since 2008 we have had the annual England Schools v MCC Schools match at Lord's, followed by a grand Dinner in the magnificent Long Room.

Last, but by no means least, the Bunbury Celebrity Cricket Team (only 7 defeats in 652 matches played) has so far raised £17 million for different charities and worthwhile causes.

Dr David English, CBE, MBE, O.S.C.A. - We salute you!

Now that we are well into the 2016 cricket season and the 30th Bunbury ESCA Festival is just around the corner, I realise that the football season is just a month away and wonder if the Gunners can win their first Premier League title in 13 years. My great friend Phil Lawrence introduced me to The Arsenal in 1996, exactly a month after Arsene Wenger became Manager.

"We're very boring and nobody likes us, but it's a nice day out at Highbury," Phil said to me 20 years ago. I saw them beat Leeds United 3-0 on 26th October 1996 and have been hooked ever since. That day they had ten Brits in their starting line-up plus Dennis Bergkamp, who has always been my favourite Arsenal player.

At the other end of the football spectrum, I am a season ticket holder at Exeter City, a lovely, well-run club, owned by the fans and with an average home gate of around 3,500. So a bit different from Arsenal's 60,000 at the Emirates. At Exeter I meet up with my great friend and colleague Ted Ashman (we both represent the South & West on the ESCA Executive) and his son Giles.

I am so pleased that England won the Six Nations Rugby (with three former Millfield pupils in the regular starting line-up) and, almost incredibly, achieving a 3-0 series win in Australia.

I've enjoyed scoring Millfield Prep's 1st XI matches (and even a thrilling U13 Girls' match on the hallowed turf) this summer; managing Somerset U11s on Sundays; managing Glastonbury U11s on Fridays; and, of course, managing the South & West at the Bunbury Festival. The seven Schools' Cup competitions have been hampered by poor weather, but we're getting there.

If ever I'm free, I'll call in at the County Ground to watch my beloved Somerset.

I've been very lucky; it's all gone pretty well so far. Enjoyed (mostly) every minute.

And I hope it may last a little while longer.

The South & West Management Team at the 2016 Bunbury Festival at Radley College
L - R: Peter Bolland, Steve Williams, and self

The four players who graduated from Somerset U10s to Bunbury Festival Winners in 2019
L - R: James Rew, Charlie Sharland, George Thomas and Jack Harding

CHAPTER 19

From Team Manager to Car Park Attendant

The 32nd Bunbury Festival took place in August 2018 at Millfield School, just seven miles from my home in Wells. It was the first to be totally organised and run by the England & Wales Cricket Board (the first 31 having been very successfully masterminded by the English Schools' Cricket Association) and would prove to be my last. As previously mentioned, the Festival returned to Somerset after a gap of 29 years.

Steve Williams has been Head Coach of the South & West Region (should be South-West & Wales Region, but there you go!) since 2010. Steve is a thoroughly decent person and a highly conscientious coach, although certainly not at his best in the administrative aspect of the job. In the years leading up to the Millfield Festival, I became more and more marginalised in the trials and warm-up matches. It wasn't until the South & West Bunbury squad of 14 players was announced each year that I really took over my role as Team Manager. The pre-Festival preparation has taken up more time in recent years with the advent of Risk Assessment, Health & Safety, Child Protection, Player Welfare, including dietary needs, etc., etc. I would occasionally do the scoring in warm-up games (if I knew about them), which I know that Steve appreciated rather more than David Graveney, the National Performance Manager. Everyone was reminded that with the England & Wales Cricket Board now funding the Bunbury Festivals, cuts of 20% had to be made. More of my thoughts on the ECB later.

After eight Bunbury Festivals with Steve Williams, Peter Bolland and myself at the helm for the South & West, Bolly was replaced/voluntarily stood down (for a reason I never quite understood) in favour of Andy Woodward, while I survived for just one more year. Bolly was, and still is, an excellent coach, while his traditional Monday night Sports Quizzes at the Festivals were always very popular. We had some great times on the West's Caribbean Tours; 2005 and that boat trip will always be remembered (by everyone who was in the boat for both crossings!), when three months later we triumphed in the Bunbury Festival at Newquay under the astute captaincy of James Harris. James made his Glamorgan debut as a 16 year-old and has now completed seven seasons at Lord's with Middlesex. Since leaving Newquay some years ago, Bolly has been doing great work at Redruth Cricket Club as coach and, I suspect, several other vital jobs. The 2019 season saw the club finish as runners-up in the Cornwall Premier League, many of the players having come up through their excellent youth programme of coaching and age-group matches. League champions were Penzance who recruited players from afar with their sizeable playing budget; as incidentally did Wiltshire club Potterne who won the West of England Premier League for the first time. Clevedon Cricket Club did much the same thing in 2018. Back to Redruth and I can report that their 2nd XI were runners-up in Division 1 of the Cornwall League, while the 3rd XI were champions of Division 4 West. So a great season all round for this thriving club.

After the almost traditional defeat to the Midlands on the opening day of the Millfield Festival, the South & West went from strength to strength, winning the remaining two 50 Over games and both T20 matches. Will Naish, as captain and all-rounder, performed very well, as did Henry Smeed who like Will had played in the 2017 Stowe Festival. Millfield's Jamie Baird was one of the two excellent keeper/batsmen, while 14 year-old James Coles produced more than expected with his batting and left-arm spinners. James turned out to be a real star turn in this year's Bunbury Festival at Felsted School, leading his side to victory in all five matches. So I wasn't missed at all! When T20 cricket started in 2003, most people (including me) thought that spinners would hardly get a look-in and that seamers would do most, if not all, of the bowling. However, this has not been the case and a number of slow bowlers have been very effective in this form of the game. Max Waller regularly bowls the first over of the innings when Somerset are in the field and once took two wickets against Sussex in so doing; not easy when, for the first six overs, only two fielders are allowed outside the circle. In the South & West's two T20 wins, our four spinners bowled 16 of the 20 overs and the opposition batsmen struggled to cope. Despite weeks of hot, sunny and dry weather, which broke on the Wednesday, the Millfield groundstaff had produced great cricket wickets but had spent hours filling in holes which had opened up on the outfield at Junior Field. In mid- May I saw Callum Harvey score a superb century there for Millfield U14s against Canford School and noted that the entire playing area was in pristine condition; after that, we had virtually no rain during the next ten weeks.

As nearly always happens when one organisation (ECB) takes over from another (ESCA) in running an event, they want to make changes, almost out of spite or with the attitude that we are the professionals and you amateurs have just been blundering along for thirty years. I have seen school Heads retire, leaving a good, happy and successful place of learning, only for their successor to come in and make wholesale and unnecessary changes almost at once. Bolly's Monday evening Quiz went (replaced by nothing), Tuesday's BBQ was moved to Wednesday and, astonishingly, was only for parents as the players had a 'mobile Nando's' about 500 yards away. So the Tuesday evening was blank as well. Up until 2016 at Radley one of the highlights of the week had been the Festival Dinner on the Thursday with speeches and presentations. This was replaced by... nothing, except that there was an ad hoc presentation on the Friday lunchtime after the T20 Finals. However, David English did present to players, coaches, managers and umpires (all under 25, which has been an excellent ECB initiative) a superbly designed and struck commemorative medal in a beautiful case. Charlie Hobden spoke movingly about the Matthew Hobden Trust and presented Jacob Bethell with the 'Player of the Festival' trophy, set up in Matthew's name.

Later in August, the South & West played the touring West Indies U16 team at Oxford Cricket Club, a fine hundred from Tom Prest enabling us to win quite comfortably. At the end of the match I was invited into the home dressing room and was presented with a 'Thank You' card and a £50 Meal Voucher to be spent at Café 21 in Wells – owned and run by my good friends Nigel and Mel Hancock. They had very kindly hosted two book signings for me in August 2016. Now, in my naivety, as it turned out, this presentation wasn't just for the 2018 season, but for thirty-two Bunbury Festivals with the West and South & West – so a thank-you, goodbye and enjoy your retirement! I had no official communication from David Graveney, Steve Williams or indeed anyone at all from the ECB, but that had become the norm. In the spring of 2019 I began receiving e-mails from Ashleigh Scott, ECB Festival Welfare Officer, setting out plans and strategies for the Bunbury Festival at Felsted; so nobody had seen fit to inform Ashleigh that I was no longer involved and had been replaced by Mark Allum from Berkshire. I did turn up to the first outdoor session of the season on May Day Monday, but only because it was at Wells Cathedral School (half a mile from my home) and because I still hadn't heard officially that I was being replaced (never have and never will). On arrival, I heard that my successor had just been 'introduced to the crowd' so to speak and after (on request) working the electric scoreboard until after 5pm for 70 overs – which I was more than happy to do – walked home, contemplating that I now had some 'cricket time' to fill.

Somewhat ironically, 2018 was also the last year I would be managing a Somerset age-group team. You will remember me saying earlier that a school head or suchlike coming into a new post invariably wishes to make his or her mark and make significant changes. Matt Drakeley was appointed as the Somerset Cricket Board's Head of Performance for the age-groups in January 2018 and from 2018-2019 introduced the Somerset Pathway scheme; most probably after some directives from the ECB. In fact, their main recommendations at U11 & U10 levels were (a) to shorten the pitches by 3 yards (yes, nine feet) from 20 to 17 yards, to enhance both skill development and player experience; (b) smaller boundaries, mainly to give players more opportunity to strike fours and sixes regardless of physical development. Yes, I can see some value in that, although bowling figures will suffer and become somewhat meaningless; and (c) flexible match-day rules to ensure that player development is maximised – field restrictions, etc, etc. I have to say, with regard to (a), that I saw the Overton twins, Craig and Jamie, bowling for Devon U10s and U11s in 2004 and 2005 (on 20 yard pitches) and they looked pretty fearsome. If they'd be bowling on 17 yard pitches (which, when you take the creases at each end into account, the batter is just about 13 yards away) I believe they could have unintentionally caused serious injury. It is also claimed that U11 spinners struggled to 'get the ball up there' on 20 yard pitches. Well, from personal experience, Jack Leach had no trouble doing this in 2002 and neither did Lachlan Rice in 2018. Incidentally, the pitch length at U13 level has been reduced from 21 to 19 yards. The captain of Millfield Prep School's 1st XI (U13) for the 2019 season was Dominic Kelly from Hampshire. Dominic is a fantastic prospect as a fine left-hand batsman and a very accurate right-arm fast bowler with a lovely action. As scorer for the team's home games during the season, I lost count of the number of times the game had to be stopped because Dominic's bowling was simply too quick, even for decent opposing batsmen. They were being struck on the body by deliveries just short of a length, often in the game's first over as Dominic invariably won the toss and inserted the opposition. The final home match was a National Bunbury semi-final (when I was the square-leg umpire) and a visiting batsman was struck just under the heart by a sickening blow. He retired hurt, bravely came back later but struggled to even move his upper body so retired again. I hope the lad isn't put off the game for life. I shall watch the future progress of Dominic Kelly, now at Millfield Senior School, with great interest. A huge talent.

So, for 2018-2019 the Somerset Pathway Centres have replaced County Age Group and District cricket at U10 and U11 levels. After preliminary trials and assessments in the autumn of 2018, 93 boys were selected to receive eleven indoor coaching sessions at various venues around the county between January and April. Each session was attended by about 24 boys, generally lasted two hours and the total cost to parents was £180. When April arrived, the outdoor playing season saw three Phases come into play.

Phase One entailed all 93 players (though some had dropped out at the outset) being involved in a minimum of four Development Days across the North and South of the county.

Phase Two saw a selected group of players identified from Phase One to participate in a series of North v South fixtures with a minimum of four match days.

Phase Three involved a selected group of players from Phase Two being invited to take part in a minimum of six fixtures 'against counties with like-minded philosophies around the development of young cricketers'.

Managers (always unpaid) were being made redundant and county age-group teams were now to be run by two coaches. Team sheets and other administrative details were sent out from 'central office'. I know for a fact that on more than one occasion only one coach was present for a county fixture, which is probably 'illegal' nowadays. Information on the Somerset Cricket Board website about age-group matches was minimal. Many of the U11 and U10 county fixtures were of the T20 variety, with everyone bowling one or two overs and being retired on reaching 20/30. When I mentioned that, at the age of seven, Daniel Bell-Drummond had scored a century for Kent U10s v Middlesex U10s, the reply that I got was that nobody else was given a chance that day! However, I was heartened to see that in their final match of the season Somerset U10s beat Gloucestershire U10s by one wicket in an exciting match of 35 overs a side. Proper cricket at last.

Exactly one quarter (six out of 24) of the 2019 Somerset professional staff started their county cricket careers in Ted Ashman's Devon U10 and U11 teams, playing other counties in 35 and 40 over matches. I know for a fact that all six – the Overton twins (Craig and Jamie), Lewis Gregory, Dom Bess, Tom Lammonby and Ben Green – will always remember with huge gratitude the fantastic opportunity Ted gave them at this young age. Proper, well organised cricket with appointed umpires and scorers on a good club or school ground and the young players arriving smartly dressed in collar and tie, grey trousers, polished black shoes, etc. Tea between the innings organised by mums and similar hospitality expected, quite rightly, at an away match. Now, I'm not talking about how things were in the good old days/dark ages (depending on your point of view), but less than twenty years ago.

So I had lost two Team Manager posts in a short space of time which, to say the least, was a touch careless. However, I was delighted to spend two and a half weeks assisting Malcolm Broad at his iconic and ever popular County Festivals at King's College in Taunton. Malcolm has been organising and running junior cricket festivals since 1983 and these at King's since 1994. That was the year I managed Somerset Schools U13s at the Festival and recall that Wesley Durston was my captain. With Wes reaching 40 in 2020, I can only reflect that the years go by far too quickly. That Festival 25 years ago was the only one at King's; this year (2019) there were ten Festivals at five different age-groups (U14 to U10) which lasted from 15th July to 21st August (see pages 121-123). Four years ago, a long serving member of the England & Wales Cricket Board thought that Malcolm's Festivals would have ended by now as there would be no need for them, counties wouldn't want to attend or their County Boards would prevent them from attending (which, sadly, Yorkshire has done). Well, I can assure this gentleman that the King's Festivals prosper more than ever and Malcolm has waiting lists at all the age-groups. You sense for all the teams that their week at King's playing 'proper' cricket is the highlight of their season. Some players in the Lancashire U14 team had been coming to King's since their U10 days and, dare I say it, were a little emotional when they realised it would be their last visit.

I assisted at the Festivals for two separate weeks, both with my ESCA colleague Richard Young. Then, with Phil Evans (London & East Team Manager), I helped at the final three days of the Festivals when there were three age-groups in residence – U13, U12, U10. Two other ESCA personnel – Mike Spinks and Richard Somerford – also assisted in other weeks of the Festivals. Having managed various Somerset teams in almost all of the first 25 years of the Festivals, it was interesting to be on the other side of the fence, so to speak. The four regular Festival staff (all youngsters!) were Tom Jayne, Ashley Bicknell, Melvin Burt and Sam Wyatt. Tom produced all the day's scorecards each evening, while all four worked extremely hard along with Malcolm to ensure the smooth running of the Festivals. I hereby thank all of them for putting up with the somewhat quirky ways (especially mine!) of the five ESCA officials. After all, some of us are around 50 years older! Fairly early on I decided I could make myself most useful between 9am and 10.30 each morning by donning a high viz jacket and directing cars at the main entrance of the King's campus to the car park nearest to where their son's team was playing. Almost without exception, I found parents very appreciative of this facility. In fact, one Cambridgeshire mum seemed close to adding me to her Christmas card list by the end of the week!

Glastonbury Cricket Club U10 Team 2019
Winners of the Mid-Wessex League Knock-Out Cup

CHAPTER 20
A Never-to-be Forgotten Cricket Season

On Tuesday 4th September 2018 I was at Lord's for the annual MCC Schools v ESCA match, ESCA winning a close contest by just 19 runs on a day in which almost 600 runs were scored and with Luke Doneathy (a state school boy from the north-east) scoring a magnificent 113 not out off 84 balls for ESCA.

It was a pleasure to watch the afternoon play with Jos Buttler who kindly kept me informed of what was happening in the (eventually tied) match between Somerset and Lancashire in Taunton; in case you're puzzled about this, Jos has a smart phone and I have a Nokia. Jos was there to present the awards after the match to the players and officials. His calendar of cricket tours, tournaments and matches in the three formats over the following twelve months was quite astonishing.

- 15th September – Finals Day for Lancashire in the T20
- October/November – England Tour to Sri Lanka, with 3 Tests, 5 ODIs, 1 T20
- December/January – Big Bash League in Australia, playing for Sydney Thunder
- January/February/March – England Tour to West Indies, with 3 Tests, 4 ODIs, 3 T20s
- April/May – Indian Premier League, playing for Rajasthan Royals
- May – Back in England, v Pakistan, 5 ODIs, 1 T20
- May/June/July – ODI World Cup
- July – Test v Ireland (for which Jos was rested!)
- August/September – 5 Test Ashes Series

Who will ever forget the final moments of the World Cup Final at Lord's on Sunday 14th July when Jos gathered the ball in his gloves and ran out Martin Guptill; all this, of course, after sharing a vital partnership with Ben Stokes in the match itself when England's innings began to subside, not to mention the fifteen runs they scored together in the super over. I have to confess that every now and then during their crucial 5th wicket stand of 110, I switched channels to watch a couple of minutes of the Djokovic v Federer Final at Wimbledon before nervously tuning back to the cricket. After it was all over, I wonder if Jos's mum Pat thought back to the days when she was the coach of his U13 team at Cheddar Cricket Club?

As if this wasn't enough excitement – who needs The Hundred? – just six weeks later we had that incredible one wicket win by England in the Ashes Test at

Headingley; and this after being bowled out for just 67 in their 1st Innings. I have the greatest admiration for Jack Leach who has overcome illness, injury, eyesight problems and action readjustment to establish himself in the England Test team. Ben Stokes could not have had a better No.11 to partner him in that unbroken stand of 76 and who will forget Jack's 92 at Lord's as a nightwatchman? Well done, Jack. You must know that you've achieved hero status when spectators turn up in Jack Leach lookalike outfits, face masks and all. It was so good to meet up with Jack's parents, Simon and Vicky, at the Taunton County Ground towards the end of the season. Both Jack and younger brother Ben came through the productive Somerset age-group system.

England's 2-2 draw in the Ashes series brought an end to the tenure of Head Coach Trevor Bayliss. Along with his trusty and highly regarded assistant, Paul Farbrace, he did a pretty good job in his quiet, unassuming way. Winning the World Cup was the obvious highlight – and had been the primary target since Bayliss took office – but it will now be the aim of his successor, Chris Silverwood, to improve our Test record. The next Ashes series in Australia is just two years away; it will come round very quickly. Before he left for home in Australia, Bayliss made some highly pertinent suggestions in a blueprint for England cricket –

1. Counties stop arguing with the ECB and work with the England team.
2. A reduction in the amount of domestic cricket played.
3. Banning touring players from playing county cricket before a Test series.
4. More patience with coaches from county chairmen and members.
5. Flatter county pitches to promote patient batting and bowling.
6. Playing 50 over cricket at the start of the summer with the Championship starting later.

Well, I have doubts about No.1, disagree with No.2 (remembering that the 18 counties are Members' clubs), definitely agree with No.3 (Marnus Labuschagne being the prime example), no comment on No.4 but totally agree with Nos.5 & 6. I will put my cards on the table when I say that the ECB would struggle to run a bath, let alone English cricket. It has wasted money in a number of ways, an example being to give Glamorgan and Hampshire £2.5m each simply because they will not be hosting Test matches in the immediate future. The Hundred (gimmicky) takes up a prime spot in the 2020 cricket calendar (mid-July to mid-August), while the County 1-Day Final has been shunted off from Lord's to Trent Bridge, having been held at the Home of Cricket since its inception in 1963. It will be interesting to see the dates for the County Championship in 2020; there will now be ten teams in Division 1 (and eight in Division 2), but still only 14 fixtures, so Somerset, for example, will play five teams twice and four teams just once. Imagine, in the Premier League, some teams having to play Manchester City and Liverpool twice, but other teams only once. A final irritation (there are more, but I'll keep quiet about those) was to allow Warwickshire to call themselves Birmingham Bears in the Vitality Blast. Why? My reply to that request would have been, 'Sorry, mate, it's a county, not a city, competition'. Thin edge of the wedge comes to mind and, of course, we see it now with The Hundred with its city based franchises. The chances of me crossing the Severn Bridge (even though the tolls have now gone!) to watch Welsh Fire in action at Cardiff are less than zero. I won't even be watching it on BBC2; more probably Brexit debates, live from the House of Commons. Unmissable.

It was so good to see Somerset triumph in the Royal London 50 Over Final at Lord's at the end of May, especially after being runners-up in ten competitions since winning the T20 at the Oval in 2005. What was also very rewarding was that eight of the Somerset team had come through the Academy/Age-Group system (five from Somerset, three from Devon), while Dom Bess from Devon was 12th Man on the day. With the 'Somerset Pathway' starting in 2018/19, it is interesting to speculate as to whether we will see the same high percentage of home grown players in ten years' time. James Hildreth and Peter Trego were the two not out batsmen when the winning runs were struck, so doubly rewarding for me. I watched the match from the top of the Lord's Pavilion with colleagues Giles Ashman and Phil Evans. Giles's father, Ted, had passed away on 11th March after a short illness and will always be greatly missed – as an inspirational Headmaster, brilliant organiser and manager of Devon junior cricket teams – as well as Regional and National ESCA competitions - and perfect gentleman in every way.

Essex, Kyle Abbott and the weather made sure that Somerset will have to wait at least one more year to win that elusive first County Championship title; a great effort nonetheless. Tom Abell is maturing as a captain all the time, taking greater responsibility and scoring good runs in all three formats of the game. Genuine congratulations to Gloucestershire on their promotion to Division 1, especially to their hard-working coach Richard Dawson and skipper Chris Dent. Chris, from North Somerset, played for the Somerset U11 team in 2002 before switching to Gloucestershire the following season. Playing for their U12 side (against Somerset) at Thornbury Cricket Club in July 2003 he scored a brilliant century! So, Somerset's loss. Ten years ago, Gloucestershire were some way behind Somerset with their age-group cricket organisation; that is certainly not the case now. I imagine that the Somerset v Gloucestershire Championship fixture will be one that will be played at both Taunton and Bristol in 2020. Apparently, in the post war years of the late forties, this fixture was regularly played over the two Bank Holiday weekends and more often than not they closed the gates on the Monday after thousands had crammed into the County Ground in Taunton or Bristol to watch live cricket. It was the same with football, as people were yearning to spectate again after the War years.

With the significant help of Heather Hall (Chair), Dave Peck (Coach) and Keith Tooze (Grounds), I was able to keep the junior section of Glastonbury Cricket Club functioning during the season. Playing in the Mid-Wessex League, the U12 team came 3rd in their division and were Cup semi-finalists. The U10 side also finished 3rd in their division, but triumphed in the K.O. Cup against Compton House.

Finally, congratulations to Castle School in Taunton who won the National Lady Taverners U13 Girls Indoor title at Lord's in May. A huge achievement for a state school and their inspirational coach Russell Jones.

CHAPTER 21
Updates and Final Thoughts

In many sports, captaincy of a team requires little more than tossing for ends and generally giving encouragement (or otherwise) to the rest of his or her team members. Cricket, of course, is totally different. When in the field – and particularly with the advent of limited overs cricket – the skipper has to consider bowling changes (are they bowling from the right end or at the right time?), field settings, the correct number of fielders inside the circle and so on. Except on major County Grounds, the scoreboard is unlikely to indicate how many overs each bowler has bowled. In my early years as Head of Cricket at Millfield Prep, I used to give the 1st XI captain a postcard numbered 1 – 25, indicating next to each number the bowler who should be delivering that over. The team often had only five decent bowlers, so this meant that one of the five had to bowl three overs from one end early on, followed by two overs from the other end later in the innings. Nowadays, things are a little easier for the captain as, for example in the King's College Festivals, the umpires keep a note of this information.

If I had to choose the best England captain in my lifetime it would be between Brian Close and Mike Brearley. They were very different characters but outstanding leaders in their own way. Sir Ian Botham has good reason to be grateful (and I'm sure still is) to both of them; Close when he captained Somerset between 1972 and 1977 and Brearley when he took over from Botham as captain for the 3rd Ashes Test in 1981 – and, as you know, the rest is history.

In 1960/61 an iconic Test series took place between Australia (led by Richie Benaud) and the West Indies (led by Frank Worrell). The series, won by Australia 2-1, was full of great batting and bowling performances and included of course the dramatic tied Test at Brisbane. Both captains were brilliantly astute leaders who always aimed to attack rather than defend. Frank Worrell was knighted in 1964 but died three years later at the tragically young age of 42. After retiring from cricket, Richie Benaud became an outstanding and much revered cricket commentator, mainly on television. It was a privilege for me to meet him at a Millfield event in 1975. He is quoted as saying, "Captaincy is 90% luck and 10% skill, but don't try it without that 10%." Wise words. A mention also for Brendan McCullum who captained New Zealand on their tour of England in 2015. Not only did he lead his side in a very positive manner, but in the ODIs he almost persuaded/cajoled England into approaching 50 over matches in a different way; much needed after the fairly disastrous World Cup campaign in Australia a few months earlier.

In my many years of managing school, club, county and regional teams I have been fortunate to be able to appoint some excellent leaders to captain the side.

However, I am going to mention just one and he is Will Smeed. Will captained my Somerset U10 team in 2012, not because he was the best player – which he was in a strong side – but because I looked on him as a natural leader. He didn't disappoint. The following season I went to watch the final match of the King's College U11 Festival where Somerset were playing Worcestershire. Somerset were coached and managed by Rob Maggs and Mike Passingham. Will was Somerset captain, lost the toss – to prove he's not perfect – and his side was asked to bat in the 40 over match. On a damp pitch, Will scored a patient, beautifully crafted half century in a total of 170-8 and then showed superb tactical acumen when Worcestershire batted. With clever bowling changes and astute field settings, he strangled the batsmen who went an incredible eighteen overs without scoring a boundary. Will didn't bowl himself, but used two or three bowlers who had lacked opportunity earlier in the Festival due to rain interrupted matches. Worcestershire fell about 50 runs short and Rob Maggs told me afterwards that he couldn't remember having a captain like Will who needed so few pre-match instructions, especially at such a young age.

Three aspects of cricket which concern me at all age-groups are injuries, warm-ups and time wasting. Well, it seems to me that rather too many injuries are actually caused by training exercises, warm-ups before a match and strength and conditioning. I do wonder about the merits and value of pre-pubescent boys doing strength and conditioning exercises, though I believe the Somerset Pathway now doesn't include it quite so much in its programme. However, I have to say that when my U11 and U10 squads had Daz Veness occasionally before a match and Zak Bess at winter sessions, the players did seem to enjoy them, Daz and Zak making them as interesting and varied as possible. Far too many young fast bowlers now seem to get injured during the season, usually with 'stress fractures'. It happens at senior level too. In August this year, England had four quick bowlers out through injury – Jimmy Anderson, Mark Wood, Ollie Stone and Tom Curran. When I used to watch Somerset in the 'sixties, opening bowlers Ken Palmer and Fred Rumsey used to bowl two or three times as many overs in a season as they do now and never seemed to get injured. I heard Alec Bedser once say that every February he received a letter from Surrey instructing him to report to the Oval on 1st April, FIT TO PLAY CRICKET. On arrival, he would bowl in the nets to get into rhythm, before sending down 1,000 + overs during the season. Back to warm-ups for junior teams and I really think they should always be cricket related and not too long, especially in hot weather, and should not include playing football on the outfield (sorry, England), jumping through hoops and doing endless exercises without a bat or ball in sight. Finally, time wasting! Keep the game moving! Cut out the slowness between overs, interminable discussions about field placings, too many drinks breaks (except, of course, on very hot days) and last, but not least, coaches giving endless team talks and debriefs. Former Millfield Prep coach/

manager Simon Wynn (2003-2017) always expected his team to bowl 20 overs an hour – which is as it should be.

I am delighted to report that two of my former Somerset U10 players – Kasey Aldridge and Sam Young – have been given two year contracts by Somerset, as has Lewis Goldsworthy of Cornwall. Lewis's father Ian was the West Region captain on the very first West Indies Tour in 1989-90. All three have just left Millfield School and will be touring the Caribbean the month before Christmas with England U19s. The aim for the three of them will be a place in the England squad for the U19 World Cup in 2020. Good luck to them all.

Will and Henry Smeed have been hampered by injuries over the past year but they remain great talents and certainly names to look out for in the next few years. After being out while recovering from a shoulder operation, Will returned to action at the end of July and promptly scored a double century for Somerset U17s. George Bartlett (another of my U10s - in 2008) established himself in the Somerset team, scoring over 700 runs in the Championship.

I have previously mentioned Dominic Kelly of Hampshire and now another Kelly to look out for is Noah Kelly of Yorkshire. Noah looked a very talented wicketkeeper/batsman playing for Yorkshire U11s in the King's Festival in 2017 and I see that he led his County U13s to success in the Northern Counties Cup this year, scoring an undefeated half century in the final against Warwickshire. Another young player showing huge promise is Kian Roberts of Taunton Prep School. Kian hails from Cornwall but is now in the Somerset system. His father David remains the record run scorer for Cornwall Schools (U11 – U17) with 3679 runs, and I imagine will always remain so.

It was very gratifying to see that four of this year's all-conquering South & West Bunbury squad played in my Somerset U10 team five years ago. They were James Rew, Charlie Sharland, George Thomas and Jack Harding. Joseph Eckland should probably have been selected too, but he was a standby reserve. So, not bad to have four chosen out of a squad of 14, selected from 12 counties and the whole of Wales.

After leaving Millfield School in 2013, Teddie Casterton spent the next four years at RGS High Wycombe. In 2017 he became the first-ever state school boy to become Wisden Schools Cricketer of the Year. Playing for and captaining a team with a competitive fixture list, Teddie scored 1423 runs at an average of almost 90. A brilliant achievement.

Outstanding rugby player Oran McNulty left Millfield in 2018 and is now in his second season at Connacht's Rugby Academy in Ireland. Younger brother Finn, now 16, is established in Millfield's 1st XV squad for 2019-2020.

I'm delighted to still be a season ticket holder at Exeter City FC. Their new stand and covered away end were completed a year ago and the ground and pitch look in great shape. Former player and fans' favourite Matt Taylor took over from Paul Tisdale as Manager in the summer of 2018 and will be striving to get the team promoted to League 1 after a near miss last season.

I make only occasional visits to watch The Arsenal, along with Phil Lawrence (who recently completed 100 terms on the staff at Port Regis) and Rufus Lacey. Rufus – now 19 and who has still never seen the Gunners lose a league match – graduated from the Swindon Dance Academy to the National Youth Dance Company and twice performed on stage at Sadler's Wells. A year ago he successfully auditioned for a part in CATS (the movie), as a Jellicle, which is due to be released in December 2019. The film features such luminaries as Dame Judi Dench, James Corden, Sir Ian McKellan, Idris Elba, Taylor Swift and Jennifer Hudson. In one sequence, Rufus has to lift Taylor Swift up into the air and I was relieved to hear that he didn't drop her!

I must conclude with David English and the Bunburys. The list of England players who are former Bunburys has now reached 95 (I think) and the Bunfather is fervently hoping that the magic 100 figure is reached over the winter. Meanwhile, Dr. Dave has recently appointed me Bunbury Director of Press, Publicity and Communications! I couldn't be more proud... as I was to receive the magnificent silver trophy from David and Ken Lake, recognising my attendance at thirty-two Bunbury Festivals. Long may they continue carrying the Bunbury name.

UNDER 14 FESTIVAL 1 and UNDER 13 FESTIVAL 1
MONDAY 15th JULY - FRIDAY 19th JULY, 2019.

DAY and DATE	PITCH 1	PITCH 2	PITCH 3	PITCH 4	PITCH 5	PITCH 6
MONDAY **15 JULY** Start: 10.30	BUCKS v OXFORD Lunch: 12.25	GLOUCESTER v SHROPSHIRE Lunch: 12.30	CRICSTAR v DEVON Lunch: 12.35	CALIFORNIA v NORTHANTS Lunch: 12.45	OXFORD v SHROPSHIRE Lunch: 12.50	CAMBRIDGE v SOMERSET Lunch: 12.55
TUESDAY **16 JULY** Start: 10.00	CRICSTAR v SHROPSHIRE Lunch: 12.25	BUCKS v DEVON Lunch: 12.30	GLOUCESTER v OXFORD Lunch: 12.35	CAMBRIDGE v SHROPSHIRE Lunch: 12.45	NORTHANTS v SOMERSET Lunch: 12.50	CALIFORNIA v OXFORD Lunch: 12.55
WEDNESDAY **17 JULY** Start: 10.00	DEVON v GLOUCESTER Lunch: 12.25	OXFORD v SHROPSHIRE Lunch: 12.30	BUCKS v CRICSTAR Lunch: 12.35	SHROPSHIRE v SOMERSET Lunch: 12.45	CALIFORNIA v CAMBRIDGE Lunch: 12.50	NORTHANTS v OXFORD Lunch: 12.55
THURSDAY **18 JULY** Start: 10.00	CRICSTAR v OXFORD Lunch: 12.25	BUCKS v GLOUCESTER Lunch: 12.30	DEVON v SHROPSHIRE Lunch: 12.35	CAMBRIDGE v NORTHANTS Lunch: 12.45	OXFORD v SOMERSET Lunch: 12.50	CALIFORNIA v SHROPSHIRE Lunch: 12.55
FRIDAY **19 JULY** Start: 10.00	BUCKS v SHROPSHIRE Lunch: 12.20	DEVON v OXFORD Lunch: 12.25	CRICSTAR v GLOUCESTER Lunch: 12.30	CALIFORNIA v SOMERSET Lunch: 12.40	CAMBRIDGE v OXFORD Lunch: 12.45	NORTHANTS v SHROPSHIRE Lunch: 12.50

UNDER 14 FESTIVAL 2 for 2019
SUNDAY 21st JULY - FRIDAY 26th JULY

DAY and DATE	PITCH 1	PITCH 2	PITCH 3	PITCH 4	PITCH 5	WYVERN
SUNDAY **21 JULY** Start: 11.00	BARBADOS v TRINIDAD Lunch: 13.00					
MONDAY **22 JULY** Start: 10.00	DURHAM v KENT Lunch: 12.25	LANCASHIRE v NOTTS Lunch: 12.30	NORFOLK v TRINIDAD Lunch: 12.35	BARBADOS v CALIFORNIA Lunch: 12.45	CHESHIRE v CORNWALL Lunch: 12.50	NORTHANTS v N. IRELAND Lunch: 12.30
TUESDAY **23 JULY** Start: 10.00	NORFOLK v NOTTS Lunch: 12.25	KENT v TRINIDAD Lunch: 12.30	DURHAM v LANCASHIRE Lunch: 12.35	CORNWALL v NORTHANTS Lunch: 12.45	CALIFORNIA v N. IRELAND Lunch: 12.50	BARBADOS v CHESHIRE Lunch: 12.30
WEDNESDAY **24 JULY** Start: 10.00	CORNWALL v N. IRELAND Lunch: 12.25	CALIFORNIA v CHESHIRE Lunch: 12.30	BARBADOS v NORTHANTS Lunch: 12.35	NOTTS v TRINIDAD Lunch: 12.45	KENT v LANCASHIRE Lunch: 12.55	DURHAM v NORFOLK Lunch: 12.30
THURSDAY **25 JULY** Start: 10.00	CALIFORNIA v NORTHANTS Lunch: 12.25	BARBADOS v CORNWALL Lunch: 12.30	CHESHIRE v N. IRELAND Lunch: 12.35	LANCASHIRE v NORFOLK Lunch: 12.45	DURHAM v TRINIDAD Lunch: 12.55	KENT v NOTTS Lunch: 12.30
FRIDAY **26 JULY** Start: 10.00	LANCASHIRE v TRINIDAD Lunch: 12.20	DURHAM v NOTTS Lunch: 12.25	KENT v NORFOLK Lunch: 12.30	BARBADOS v N. IRELAND Lunch: 12.40	CHESHIRE v NORTHANTS Lunch: 12.50	CALIFORNIA v CORNWALL Lunch: 12.30

UNDER 13 FESTIVALS 2 and 3 2019

DAY and DATE	PITCH 1	PITCH 2	PITCH 3	PITCH 4	PITCH 5	PITCH 6
MONDAY 29 JULY Start: 10.30	AMERICA ACAD v NORFOLK Lunch: 12.25	CUMBRIA v WORCESTER Lunch: 12.30	DEVON v LANCASHIRE Lunch: 12.35	CHESHIRE v LEICESTER Lunch: 12.45	KENT v HAMPSHIRE Lunch: 12.50	CORNWALL v LONDON Lunch: 12.55
TUESDAY 30 JULY Start: 10.00	DEVON v WORCESTER Lunch: 12.25	AMERICA ACAD v LANCASHIRE Lunch: 12.30	CUMBRIA v NORFOLK Lunch: 12.35	HAMPSHIRE v LONDON Lunch: 12.45	CHESHIRE v CORNWALL Lunch: 12.50	KENT v LEICESTER Lunch: 12.55
WEDNESDAY 31 JULY Start: 10.00	CHESHIRE v LONDON Lunch: 12.25	CORNWALL v KENT Lunch: 12.30	LEICESTER v HAMPSHIRE Lunch: 12.35	DEVON v AMERICA ACAD Lunch: 12.45	CUMBRIA v LANCASHIRE Lunch: 12.50	NORFOLK v WORCESTER Lunch: 12.55
THURSDAY 1 AUGUST Start: 10.00	CORNWALL v LEICESTER Lunch: 12.25	CHESHIRE v HAMPSHIRE Lunch: 12.30	KENT v LONDON Lunch: 12.35	DEVON v NORFOLK Lunch: 12.45	LANCASHIRE v WORCESTER Lunch: 12.50	CUMBRIA v AMERICA ACAD Lunch: 12.55
FRIDAY 2 AUGUST Start: 10.00	LANCASHIRE v NORFOLK Lunch: 12.20	AMERICA ACAD v WORCESTER Lunch: 12.25	CUMBRIA v DEVON Lunch: 12.30	CORNWALL v HAMPSHIRE Lunch: 12.40	LEICESTER v LONDON Lunch: 12.45	CHESHIRE v KENT Lunch: 12.50

UNDER 11 FESTIVALS 1 AND 2 - 2019

SUNDAY 4th AUGUST - FRIDAY 9th AUGUST

DAY and DATE	PITCH 1	PITCH 2	PITCH 3	PITCH 4	PITCH 5	PITCH 6
MONDAY 5 AUGUST Start: 10.30	CAMBRIDGE v DEVON Lunch: 12.25	CHESHIRE v WORCESTER Lunch: 12.30	GLOUCESTER v NOTTS Lunch: 12.35	CORNWALL v LEICESTER Lunch: 12.45	CALIFORNIA v KENT Lunch: 12.50	LANCASHIRE v OXFORD Lunch: 12.55
TUESDAY 6 AUGUST Start: 10.30	NOTTS v WORCESTER Lunch: 12.25	DEVON v GLOUCESTER Lunch: 12.30	CAMBRIDGE v CHESHIRE Lunch: 12.35	KENT v OXFORD Lunch: 12.45	CORNWALL v LANCASHIRE Lunch: 12.50	CALIFORNIA v LEICESTER Lunch: 12.55
WEDNESDAY 7 AUGUST Start: 10.30	KENT v LANCASHIRE Lunch: 12.25	CALIFORNIA v CORNWALL Lunch: 12.30	LEICESTER v OXFORD Lunch: 12.35	DEVON v WORCESTER Lunch: 12.45	CAMBRIDGE v GLOUCESTER Lunch: 12.50	CHESHIRE v NOTTS Lunch: 12.55
THURSDAY 8 AUGUST Start: 10.30	CORNWALL v OXFORD Lunch: 12.25	KENT v LEICESTER Lunch: 12.30	CALIFORNIA v LANCASHIRE Lunch: 12.35	CAMBRIDGE v NOTTS Lunch: 12.45	CHESHIRE v DEVON Lunch: 12.50	GLOUCESTER v WORCESTER Lunch: 12.55
FRIDAY 9 AUGUST Start: 10.00	CHESHIRE v GLOUCESTER Lunch: 12.20	DEVON v NOTTS Lunch: 12.25	CAMBRIDGE v WORCESTER Lunch: 12.30	CALIFORNIA v OXFORD Lunch: 12.40	LANCASHIRE v LEICESTER Lunch: 12.45	CORNWALL v KENT Lunch: 12.50

UNDER 12 FESTIVALS 1 and 2 2019

MONDAY 12th AUGUST - FRIDAY 16th AUGUST

DAY and DATE	PITCH 1	PITCH 2	PITCH 3	PITCH 4	PITCH 5	PITCH 6
MONDAY 12 AUGUST Start: 10.00	DEVON v GLOUCESTER Lunch: 12.25	HAMPSHIRE v LANCASHIRE Lunch: 12.30	CALIFORNIA v SOMERSET Lunch: 12.35	BARBADOS v NOTTS Lunch: 12.45	CORNWALL v DORSET Lunch: 12.50	WALES v WORCESTER Lunch: 12.55
TUESDAY 13 AUGUST Start: 10.00	CALIFORNIA v HAMPSHIRE Lunch: 12.25	DEVON v SOMERSET Lunch: 12.30	GLOUCESTER v LANCASHIRE Lunch: 12.35	DORSET v WORCESTER Lunch: 12.45	CORNWALL v NOTTS Lunch: 12.50	BARBADOS v WALES Lunch: 12.55
WEDNESDAY 14 AUGUST Start: 10.00	BARBADOS v CORNWALL Lunch: 12.25	NOTTS v WORCESTER Lunch: 12.30	DORSET v WALES Lunch: 12.35	CALIFORNIA v LANCASHIRE Lunch: 12.45	DEVON v HAMPSHIRE Lunch: 12.50	GLOUCESTER v SOMERSET Lunch: 12.55
THURSDAY 15 AUGUST Start: 10.00	NOTTS v WALES Lunch: 12.25	BARBADOS v DORSET Lunch: 12.30	CORNWALL v WORCESTER Lunch: 12.35	HAMPSHIRE v SOMERSET Lunch: 12.45	CALIFORNIA v GLOUCESTER Lunch: 12.50	DEVON v LANCASHIRE Lunch: 12.55
FRIDAY 16 AUGUST Start: 10.00	LANCASHIRE v SOMERSET Lunch: 12.25	GLOUCESTER v HAMPSHIRE Lunch: 12.20	CALIFORNIA v DEVON Lunch: 12.30	CORNWALL v WALES Lunch: 12.40	BARBADOS v WORCESTER Lunch: 12.45	DORSET v NOTTS Lunch: 12.50

UNDER 13 FESTIVAL 4, UNDER 12 FESTIVAL 3 and UNDER 10 FESTIVAL

SUNDAY 18th AUGUST - WEDNESDAY 21st AUGUST, 2019.

DAY and DATE	PITCH 1	PITCH 2	PITCH 3	PITCH 4	PITCH 5	PITCH 6
SUNDAY 18 AUGUST Start: 15.00	Under 12 CORNWALL v SOMERSET Start: 11.30 Lunch: 13.00				Under 10 CHESHIRE v LANCASHIRE T20	Under 10 BERKSHIRE v CORNWALL T20
MONDAY 19 AUGUST Start: 10.30	Under 13 CORNWALL v GLOUCESTER Lunch: 12.25	Under 12 CORNWALL v LEICESTER Lunch: 12.30	Under 13 GLOUCS U14 DEV v SUFFOLK Lunch: 12.35	Under 12 ESSEX v WILTSHIRE Lunch: 12.45	Under 10 CHESHIRE v LANCASHIRE Lunch: 12.50	Under 10 BERKSHIRE v CORNWALL Lunch: 12.55
TUESDAY 20 AUGUST Start: 10.00	Under 13 CORNWALL v SUFFOLK Lunch: 12.45	Under 12 LEICESTER v ESSEX Lunch: 12.30	Under 13 GLOUCESTER v GLOUCS U14 DEV Lunch: 12.35	Under 12 CORNWALL v WILTSHIRE Lunch: 12.45	Under 10 CORNWALL v LANCASHIRE Lunch: 12.50	Under 10 BERKSHIRE v CHESHIRE Lunch: 12.55
WEDNESDAY 21 AUGUST Start: 10.00	Under 13 CORNWALL v GLOUCS U14 DEV Lunch: 12.20	Under 12 CORNWALL v ESSEX Lunch: 12.35	Under 13 GLOUCESTER v SUFFOLK Lunch: 12.25	Under 12 LEICESTER v WILTSHIRE Lunch: 12.40	Under 10 BERKSHIRE v LANCASHIRE Lunch: 12.45	Under10 CORNWALL v CHESHIRE Lunch: 12.50

INDEX OF NAMES

Broad, Malcolm - 71, 72, 73, 95, 96, 101, 111
Brock, Tom - 53
Brocklehurst, Ben - 104
Brogan, Dominic - 24
Bull, Leslie - 12
Burgess, Graham - 84
Burt, Melvin - 112
Buttler, Jos - 61, 101, 113
    Pat - 113
Buzza, Alan - 95

Cabble, Pete - 40
Cameron, David - 83
Cartwright, Tom - 102
Casey, Liam - 29
Casterton, Teddie - 56, 119
Chalke, George - 49
    Georgie - 49
    Mel - 49
Champion, Sarah - 30, 62
Chapman, Chris - 49
Chapple, Glen - 99
Cheney, Kevin - 42
Cherry, Hugh - 102
Chopra, Varun - 39
Churches, Craig - 35
Churchill, Sir Winston - 72
Clayton, Darren - 36
Cleese, John - 103
Close, Brian - 117
Close, Dan - 68
Clough, Dr Fran - 68
Coates, Stuart - 31, 32, 59
Cocks, Daryl - 90
Coles, James - 108
Coles, Johnny - 16
Collingwood, Paul - 100
Collins, Chantal - 69
Cook, Sir Alastair - 37
Cook, Jimmy - 92
Cooper, Cyril - 98, 104

Cope, Dean - 21
Corden, James - 120
Corner, Tony - 27
Cottam, Bob - 85
Cowdrey, Chris - 37
Craddock, Roger - 99
Crane, Will - 92
Crawley, John - 98
Cullinan, Juliet - 81
Cummins, Simon - 31, 33, 34, 35, 36, 37, 38, 59
Curran, Tom - 118
Curtis, Andy - 84, 89, 91

Dando, Angela - 17
    Glyn - 22
Davey, John - 89
Davis, Adie - 45
Davis, Mark - 80, 84
Davis, Noah - 92
Davis, Steve - 33, 90
Davies, Haydn - 89
Davies, Tony - 91
Dawson, Richard - 101, 115
Day, Derek - 96, 97, 98, 101
Debbi (Eric Purchase Photography) - 64
Dench, Dame Judi - 120
Denning, Peter - 84
Dent, Chris - 115
Derrick, Bradley - 43
Derrick, John - 102
Dibble, Jodie - 53
Dilley, Graham - 101
Dimdore-Miles, Georgia - 67
Djokovic, Novak - 113
Doggart, Hubert - 97
Dolan, Lauren - 67
Doneathy, Luke - 113
Downes, Oliver - 23
Drakeley, Matt - 102, 109
Drew, Alex - 81
Duckett, Ben - 41, 54

Spurway, Sam - 90
Stableford, Grace - 67
Steel, Cameron - 51, 53, 55
Steer, Frank - 84
Stenner, Karen - 65
Stepney, Alex - 10
Stevens, John - 95, 96
Stewart, Alec - 100
Stokes, Ben - 113, 114
Stokes, Luke - 33
      Richard - 33
Stokes, Simon - 35
Stone, Ollie - 118
Straffen, John - 1
Suddaby, Mark - 57
Suppiah, Arul - 37
Sutton, Luke - 86, 100
Swann, Graeme - 100
Swift, Taylor - 120

Taplin, Josh - 33, 34, 59
Tate, Andy - 24, 62
Taylor, Gareth - 18
Taylor, Matt - 120
Taylor, Phil - 16
Taylor, Tim - 64
Thakor, Shiv - 61
Thomas, Clive - 59
Thomas, Don - 12
Thomas, George - 106, 119
Thomas, Henry - 101
Thomas, Josh - 92
Thompson, Ian - 81
Timms, Richard - 34, 35
Tisdale, Paul - 18, 120
Tomlins, Keith - 101
Tooze, Keith - 116
Townsend, Peter - 13, 14
Trego, Peter - 101, 103, 115
Trescothick, Marcus - 99
Troughton, James, - 100
Troughton, Patrick - 100

Truelove, Roger - 94
Trump, Harvey - 96, 97, 98
Tucker, Keith - 5
Tuckwell, Janette - 25, 78
      Steve - 78
Tudor, Alex - 100
Twort, Kay - 1
      Nev - 1
      Richard - 1, 67, 103

Vaughan, Michael - 99
Veness, Daz - 118
Verheyen, Charles - 72
Verney, Mick - 96
Vic (Tony Adams' driver) - 61
Vickery - Charlie - 53, 81
      Julie - 53
      Mark - 53
Vince, James - 102
Walker, Matthew - 98
Waller, Jack - 47
      Max - 29, 41, 54, 90, 108
Walters, Nick - 95
Ward, David - 57
Ward, Mike - 86, 99
Warren, Russell - 98
Webber, Roger - 4, 5
Weitzel, John - 94
Wells, Tom - 63
Wenger, Arsene - 15, 18, 68, 105
West, Bryan - 63
Weston, Mike - 99
      Robin - 99
White, Danny - 28
      John - 28
      John Simon - 28
White, Duncan - 50
Wickham, Paul - 85, 86, 87, 89, 99
Willey, David - 43
Williams, Gerry - 11
Williams, Graham - 102
Williams, JPR - 4